Women of El Salvador

Marilyn Thomson

Dedication

To Marianella García-Villas, President of El Salvador Commission for Human Rights, who was assassinated on the 14th March, 1983 for her work in defence of human rights.

Women of El Salvador

The Price of Freedom

Marilyn Thomson

sponsored by
**Comisión de Derechos Humanos
de El Salvador**

ISHI

**Institute for the Study
of Human Issues**
Philadelphia

Women of El Salvador was sponsored by the
Comisión de Derechos Humanos de El Salvador (CDHES)
(non-governmental), Cerrada de Otoño No. 41,
Col Escandón, México 11800, D.F., and first published by
Zed Books Ltd., 57 Caledonian Road, London N1 9BU, UK,
with support from War on Want, Three Castles House,
1 London Bridge Street, London SE1 9SG, in 1986.

This edition for the USA and Canada was published by
ISHI, Institute for the Study of Human Issues,
210 South 13th Street, Philadelphia, PA 19107, USA,
in 1986.

Cover designed by Jacque Solomons.
Printed in the United Kingdom at The Bath Press, Avon.

Library of Congress Cataloging-in-Publication Data

Thomson, Marilyn.
  The women of El Salvador.

  Bibliography: p.
  1. Women — El Salvador — Social conditions.
2. Women — El Salvador — Economic conditions.
3. El Salvador — Politics and government —
1979-   .   I. Institute for the Study of Human
Issues.   II. Title.
HQ1497.T46   1986   305.4'2'097284   86-7364

ISBN 0-89727-071-1
ISBN 0-89727-073-8 (pbk.)

Publishers' Note

Many people have worked hard to make this book possible. In particular, the Publishers would like to thank the CDHES which helped make available so much important information on human rights violations generally, and the problems of Salvadorean women specifically; the author who undertook the investigation and patiently drafted and redrafted the text; and Mandy Macdonald of the El Salvador Human Rights Committee who wrote the up-to-date account of recent developments in El Salvador since the election of President Duarte. It ought perhaps to be added that readers should bear in mind that the author took careful account of the views and advice offered by CDHES and others who read early drafts of her manuscript; nevertheless, in its present form, the book should not be taken as representing necessarily the views of the CDHES.

Author's Note

For security reasons, it has been decided to alter the names of the majority of women interviewed. Only those names which appear in full with a surname have not been altered.

Contents

Acknowledgements

To all the Salvadorean women who have contributed to this work, in particular Ana Gilma, Alicia, Argentina, Beatriz, Cecilia, Elisa, Gabriela, Elena, Ileana, Julia, Juanita, Liliam, Luz, Maria Candelaria, Maria Luisa, Magdalena, Margarita, Marta, Mercedes, Michelle, Sandra, Violeta, Yolanda and especially to the memory of Sonia López, who so clearly expressed the cause of all Salvadorean women.

To the brigade of back-up support, in particular Annette, Biddy, Daryl, Gabriela, Jacky, Marcos, Margaret, Miguel Angel, Morna, Peter, Rosco, Sonja, Terry, Ulrica.

Very special thanks to Lyn Geary, who lived it and everyone who waited . . .

We thank Oxfam-Mexico and War on Want for their generous financial assistance towards travel expenses.

Preface

The people of El Salvador are at the moment engaged in the hard and bitter defence of their right to self-determination, their right to form a popular democracy free from foreign intervention. They are fighting a war against an exceptionally voracious and brutal oligarchy which through electoral fraud and vicious repression has denied all possibility of peaceful change through democratic channels.

The resolve of Salvadorean women to involve themselves in this war is outstanding on all accounts. Whether campesinos, domestics, church women or professionals, women are organizing for immediate demands and giving support to the *Frente Democrático Revolucionario/Frente Farabundo Martí para la Liberación Nacional* (FDR-FMLN), the political and military fronts formed in 1980 around a common platform of democratic demands.

This book provides some information about women's lives and the different ways in which they have become involved in the opposition movement. It seeks to show how the present regime brutally represses women who try peacefully to organize to improve the quality of their lives.

Published information is censored and very limited. Official statistics can prove out of date, deliberately misleading or may omit women altogether. The information presented here is largely based on interviews with Salvadorean women. Some were carried out during a far too brief visit to El Salvador and Nicaragua in the spring of 1983; most are with women living in exile in Mexico and were undertaken over a period of 18 months.

The original idea came from Marianella García-Villas, the late President of the Commission for Human Rights of El Salvador (CDHES), who invited me to undertake the research in co-ordination with members of the CDHES. Marianella believed that an account of Salvadorean women's lives should emphasize how women's rights are violated within the context of the wholesale violation of all civil, socio-economic, cultural and human rights in El Salvador. Her assassination at the hands of the Salvadorean army was an immense human and political tragedy, and I am among many who have lost a friend and adviser. Marianella's inspiration, enthusiasm and guidance should have been an integral part of this book.

Marilyn Thomson
Mexico City

1 Introduction

The great majority of Salvadorean women live in conditions of abject poverty. They are predominantly campesina women, *mestizas*, of mixed Spanish and indigenous descent. Their lives have always been circumscribed by child-bearing, sickness and heavy work.

Since the beginning of the civil war in 1979, Salvadorean women have had to cope with the additional and over-riding problem of the daily and horrifying levels of human rights atrocities. In rural areas, whole communities have been destroyed in counter-insurgency operations and the few survivors, usually women and children, have been forced to move into safer areas. Women live in constant fear that they, or someone close to them, will be picked up by the security forces. Night-time is the worst. There is an unofficial curfew throughout the country, while the army and security forces patrol the streets, breaking into houses to detain, torture or murder their chosen victims, sometimes leaving corpses in the gutter or one of the now notorious rubbish pits around the capital.

There are few women who have not personally suffered the loss of some relative, friend or neighbour at the hands of the army, the government security forces or the paramilitary groups controlled by the government. Many have witnessed brutal murders, discovered mutilated corpses or have relatives detained in clandestine interrogation and torture centres.

Salvadorean women are in mourning for their murdered and disappeared. They are in mourning for their homes and in mourning for life. Between the 15 October 1979 coup and December 1983, the CDHES recorded 49,162 civilian assassinations and 3,896 disappeared. Since October 1979, therefore, 1 out of every 100 Salvadoreans has been murdered or disappeared; some 200 civilian assassinations have taken place every week.

The CDHES has no reliable record for the numbers of people who have been detained and tortured, subsequently to be released. They suggest that in almost 90% of assassinations, the victim is subjected to severe torture. Nor can the figures for assassinations be very precise, particularly from 1982 onwards, when the armed forces began to carry out regular, full-scale bomb attacks on civilian communities, using

1

Table 1.1   Salvadorean Refugees (Internal and External)

Each hour 31 Salvadoreans are forced to leave the country and 10 become internal refugees.

15 October 1979 to 30 December 1982

Internal Refugees: 300,000 (60% are under 14 years of age)
External Refugees:

Belize	7,000	Mexico	250,000
Costa Rica	10,000	Nicaragua	25,000
Guatemala	70,000	Panama	1,500
Honduras	32,000	USA	500,000

(70% are under 14 years of age)

By December 1983 there will be an estimated 1 million external refugees and half a million internal refugees.

Source: CDHES, December 1982

chemical substances such as white phosphorous. The numbers of civilian victims of these bomb attacks are often unknown, but in 1982 there were 111 recorded bomb raids on civilian communities and in 1983 this figure reached 227.

Over one-fifth of the total population in El Salvador are either internal or external refugees. The CDHES estimates that in December 1983 there were some 500,000 internal refugees and 1 million Salvadoreans in exile, the great majority victims of the violence. These refugees are mainly women with children, who live in exceptionally difficult conditions and must bear the constant anxiety of not knowing what has happened to those they have left behind (Table 1.1).

The root cause of this political repression lies in the concentration of land and power in the hands of a tiny percentage of the population. El Salvador is a small Central American republic with a population of slightly over 5 million. It remains a predominantly agricultural society with subsistence farming representing the main source of livelihood. The industrial and service sector accounts for only 20% of GNP. While it is the most densely populated country in Central America (505 inhabitants per square mile), some 60% of all cultivated lands are owned by only 2% of the population. The top 8% enjoy 50% of national income while 58% of the population earn less than 10 dollars per month per capita and 80% of the rural population earn under US$20 per month.

The monopolization of land arose from the introduction of coffee for the export market at the turn of the century, which began the transformation of land from subsistence farm holdings to large plantations. With the introduction of further export crops, mainly cotton and sugar cane, this trend has accelerated. Thousands of families have been turned off their lands and forced onto a highly unstable and insufficient labour market. Today over 40% of El Salvador's rural population is landless and 90% of all land tenures are so small that they are unable to sustain the subsistence needs of an average family.

Landless campesinos have moved into San Salvador and the new industrial sectors have failed to absorb the growing workforce. The numbers of self-employed in petty commerce, basically a form of disguised unemployment, have tripled since 1960. In rural areas, the slack agricultural seasons find more than half the population unemployed.

Over the last 50 years, the Salvadorean military and the oligarchy have controlled the government and have severely repressed any opposition to their rule. The military made their definitive entrance into politics in 1932, when General Maximilian Hernández Martínez saw fit to settle the Farabundo Martí campesino uprising by massacring an estimated 30,000 people in the space of under a week. This was the last serious challenge to oligarchic rule until the 1970s. Through the creation of an official governing party, first the PRUD and then the PCN, democratic forms were maintained, allowing for presidential elections every five years, but votes were rigged to ensure the nominated candidate's victory; opposition political leaders were detained or forced to flee the country.

Salvadorean governments over this period have been little short of military dictatorships, ruling by force and not by the consent of the people. In rural areas, the large landowners, *caciques*, maintain their own private vigilante forces and are relatively undisturbed by the rule of law. Under the Alliance for Progress, there was some attempt to 'modernize' El Salvador and improve the distribution of wealth, but with very little result. Salvadorean governments continued to pay scant attention to the needs of the poor. Slum areas in the cities are correctly called the *zonas marginalizadas*, the marginalized zones, which the government simply prefers to ignore. Some 45% of San Salvador's population live in districts where houses are at best made of corrugated iron but mostly consist of cardboard boxes and bits of scrap metal, which serve for walls. The roads are unpaved, sanitation and rubbish disposal provisions are almost non-existent, water a few blocks away and expensive. In rural areas, large families live crowded into straw or bamboo huts with mud floors. They cook on open fires and use water from the nearest stream. Any form of sanitation, piped water or electricity is virtually unknown.

Good health remains the prerogative of the elite. With only 15% of the population enjoying drinking water in the home, gastro-enteritic diseases are the first cause of death. Most Salvadorean women can expect that at least one of their children will die young and that the rest will be under-nourished. Infant mortality figures are among the highest in Latin America and one out of every five children dies before reaching the age of five. Three-quarters of all children under the age of five suffer from some degree of malnutrition.

In the 1970s, a broad opposition movement with a programme of moderate reforms, the UNO, won both the 1972 and 1977 elections but was prevented from taking power through scarcely concealed military coups and violent repression. As a result of the evident failure of an electoral strategy, the armed revolutionary movement, founded at the beginning of the decade, attracted more and more support. At the same time, a number of mass organizations, known as the popular organizations, were founded. Some are linked to the various armed liberation groups and they have successfully drawn together widely diverse sectors of Salvadorean society on a common platform. While neither strictly a political party, nor a federation of trade unions, these popular organizations were enormously important in the mobilization of civilian protest against oligarchic rule.

On 15 October 1979, a pre-emptive coup with US backing overthrew the incumbent president, General Carlos Humberto Romero. After the triumph of the Sandinistas in Nicaragua against the Somoza dictatorship, in July 1979, the US became increasingly concerned about the political stability of El Salvador. The new military-civilian junta, which included the Christian Democrat Party, was presented by the Carter administration as reformist and centrist, but political repression increased and the army maintained real control over the government. The National Guard was responsible for 86 murders and 200 wounded on the 28 October during a demonstration to demand respect for human rights, only the first of many such examples. Strikes were forcibly broken up and a number of unionists killed. Over 1,000 civilians were assassinated in the space of ten weeks and in January 1980 a large number of civilian reformers, including Christian and Social Democrats, left the new junta in protest against the continuing human rights violations.

The decimated junta tried to rally support by implementing one of the fundamental demands of the revolutionary opposition – agrarian reform. However, the three-stage scheme, announced in March 1980 and designed by the US adviser who had carried out the US programme in Vietnam, hardly got off the ground. Instead, the reform was conducted under a state of siege, imposed a day after the reform was announced, and was used as an excuse for a virtual army invasion of the countryside to destroy the campesino organizations.

The FDR–FMLN, formed in the spring of 1980, is a broad coalition of political forces including many civilian members of the juntas who resigned. It has received support from many Western and Latin American countries and from the Socialist International. The FDR–FMLN now controls over one-quarter of national territory and have repeatedly called for a negotiated solution to the conflict. The FDR called for abstention in the March 1982 elections on the grounds that,

The Democratic Revolutionary Front's Programme (FDR–FMLN)

The Democratic Revolutionary Front (FDR) was formed in April 1980 and comprises a broad spectrum of political views. A coalition of more than 20 organizations, political parties, labour federations and mass fronts, it is presently headed by the leader of the Social Democrats, Guillermo Ungo. The FDR has repeatedly called for a negotiated solution to the civil war, and has won government recognition from Mexico and France. It receives broad support from the Socialist International. The FDR includes dissident Christian Democrats, most of whom resigned from their party in the period October 1979 to March 1980, the Social Democrats and the National Democratic Union (UDN), independent professionals and intellectuals and the mass popular organizations. The great majority of the Salvadorean church community gives its support to the FDR. Many of the leaders of the FDR are ex-government ministers who resigned in abhorrence at army repression of unarmed civilians: Rubén Zamora, Minister to the Presidency in the first junta, Jorge Villacorta, Sub-Secretary for Agriculture in the first and second juntas, Oscar Menjívar, Sub-Secretary for the Economy in the first junta, Héctor Dada, Minister for Foreign Affairs in the first and second juntas, and others.

The FDR–FMLN programme describes itself as 'popular, democratic and anti-oligarchic'. Its immediate objectives are to overthrow the military dictatorship and put an end to the political, economic and social power of the small elite controlling El Salvador today.

It calls for:

1. The nationalization of the banking and financial system, foreign trade and the major utilities, such as electricity.
2. A wide-reaching agrarian reform to 'benefit the great majority of poor and middle campesinos and agricultural wage workers, and to promote the development of agriculture and cattle-raising', but without affecting the interests of the small and medium landowner.
3. An urban reform of real estate ownership, again without harming the interests of medium and small real estate owners.
4. Support to small- and medium-sized business owners.
5. A number of improvements in the social wage, including social security, education, health care and public housing.
6. Support for the popular economy through wage indexing and public subsidies for basic goods and services.

The programme concludes:

> Since 15 October 1979, various parties and sectors have vainly attempted to use the government to carry out a large part of

these measures we propose without first overthrowing the old reactionary and repressive powers and without installing a truly revolutionary and popular power. This experience has clearly confirmed that only the united revolutionary movement in alliance with all democratic forces can carry out such a work of transformation.

The FDR–FMLN programme calls for the dissolution of all the repressive security forces and the building of a new army which would include democratic forces within the existing army. The FDR–FMLN would respect all human rights and would become a member of the Non-Aligned Movement. On the basis of a mixed economy, priority would be given to the campesino and working classes, and to the creation of greater self-sufficiency with an industrial base relevant to the country's needs. It emphasizes the need for the devolution of power, through a new constitutional framework allowing for broad political participation, and the widest consultation to be achieved through education for informed decision-making.

given the repressive political climate and the history of electoral fraud, they could not be assured of genuinely free elections. Events confirmed their position. Despite heavy fines for not voting, both the extreme right-wing party, ARENA, and the Christian Democrats had to resort to conspicuous ballot box stuffing to gain a respectable result. The new provisional president, Alvaro Magaña, was eventually appointed to head a government of national unity after much pressure from the US embassy.

The Reagan administration claims that the present government represents a middle way between the extremes of right and left. However, international humanitarian agencies have repeatedly stated that the right-wing paramilitary death squads, including the rural vigilante corps, ORDEN, are working on behalf of the government and that they are usually members of the security forces who 'merely change their clothes' (see Table 1.2).

Table 1.2

Assassinated Civilians	
1979 [a]	1,149
1980	13,194
1981	16,376
1982	12,617
1983	5,826
Total	*49,162*

[a] From 15 October to 31 December

Source: CDHES, December 1983

Soldier takes up a defensive position during battle with guerilla forces in Cuscatancingo, San Salvador, on election day. Six soldiers and one guerilla girl fighter were killed.
Mike Goldwater

Mike Goldwater

Women sweep the street after 5 days of intense fighting between the army and guerillas, Usulatan.

There is no doubt that the present government would have collapsed long ago were it not for continued and massive aid from the United States. The Salvadorean army is largely composed of enforced conscripts and morale is reported as very low. Many soldiers prefer to surrender rather than to continue to fight as they know the FMLN respects the Geneva War Convention and therefore returns all prisoners of war.

The United States is now supporting El Salvador with one of the largest aid budgets of any Latin American country. The Salvadorean army is being financed and trained by the USA and US military advisers are taking part in combat missions. Honduras has been virtually transformed into a US military base from which the US is co-ordinating attacks on both El Salvador and Nicaragua.

Reagan has justified this policy on the grounds that the revolutionary forces in El Salvador and the Nicaraguan government are controlled by the Soviet Union and Cuba – therefore Central America represents a vital national security issue. The US has not been able to produce any confirmed evidence of this intervention, but has nevertheless launched a massive international and internal campaign to win support for this point of view.

Nicaragua is a member of the Non-Aligned Movement and has consistently stated that it is not prepared to accept foreign bases in its territory. It has pursued an independent development policy giving attention to the basic needs of the majority of the population and it is perhaps this successful development model, more than anything else, which threatens US interests in the area. The FDR–FMLN platform and the social and economic organization of the controlled zones also place emphasis on basic needs. For the first time, El Salvador is in a position to develop a possible alternative to the economic and political model of the oligarchy. But this possibility is being blocked by US support for a regime which maintains control through political repression.

In the past, during periods of social discontent, small numbers of women have either participated directly in the political opposition or have formed women's support organizations. In the 1930s, during the revolutionary period which followed the 1929 crash, Salvadorean women fought in Nicaragua with Augusto Sandino's Liberation army and in El Salvador, Campesina Women's Committees were formed to aid the Farabundo Martí uprising.

Women have participated in the mass opposition movement since its formation in the early 1970s. Through the work of the Popular Church, women have acquired the moral conviction that no self-respecting Christian can remain passive or distanced from the social and political problems confronting their country. Women have joined trade unions, campesino, student or professional organizations, only to find their legitimate demands ignored, their leaders and members captured or killed. In the popular organizations, women have developed wider political commitments and support the armed revolutionary movement directly.

At first it tended to be young women, particularly university and secondary school students without family responsibilities, who became politically involved in significant numbers. The expansion of the state university, the University of El Salvador (UES) and the foundation of the Catholic University (UCA) in the early 1960s meant that, for the first time, women gained access to higher education. The radical student movement, which has a history dating back to the 1920s, has been instrumental in the formation of the popular organizations and many women student lawyers and doctors have decided that only with a revolutionary change of government can their professional skills be of any use.

In the late 1970s, as sons, daughters and husbands fell victim to the repression, women of all generations have joined the revolutionary movement. One of the particular features of the popular organizations which support the FDR–FMLN is precisely the large numbers of women activists. El Salvador is a traditional and highly machista society where there are huge cultural and practical impediments working against women's political involvement. However, all the organizations which make up the FDR–FMLN have adopted a deliberate policy of recruiting women. In part, of course, stemming from the need to maximize resources, this is also a principled position based on the firm belief that a popular democracy cannot be formed without taking into account the marginalized position of women and the need to work towards ending this situation.

Finally, and relatively recently, women have begun to organize around their own demands, recognizing that these can only be met under a new government which respects the individual. An authoritarian repressive government must first be replaced by a democratic participative government before women can hope to achieve any serious advances. In part reflecting increasing contact with the women's movement abroad and the general upsurge of interest in women's issues in the Third World, the Salvadorean women's organizations have primarily developed from self-perceived necessity. While they have organized around the need for basic services, child-care facilities, their right to participate outside the home in community politics, they have mainly concentrated on educational and political work to support the FDR–FMLN. Some groups, however, are beginning to think of the future and the need to form an integrated policy for women, including such areas as sexual education, to give women more control over their own lives. In the controlled zones, where the FDR–FMLN have successfully ousted the armed forces and created their own forms of civil society, women's associations and committees have been given representation in the new local governments.

It is the possibility of improving the quality of their lives, through a popular government's community programmes, that has led men and women to support the FDR–FMLN. They have been forced to take up arms because the democratic alternative has repeatedly been denied them. And in many ways, it will be Salvadorean women who will receive the most benefit from the revolution: at present, they are the most exploited group and their needs the most ignored. Salvadorean women need both financial aid and political support – international solidarity is vital.

Part 1: No Woman's Land

2 Women and Work

Life in the country is pure work and women are just as exploited as men.
Yolanda, San Salvador, April 1983

The levels of exploitation to which the majority of Salvadoreans are subjected are sometimes hard to believe. They work incredibly long hours with no day of rest for a monthly income which in the United States would not even amount to a basic daily wage. Women are up well before dawn and may have only five or six hours sleep a night in the effort to make ends meet. Whether engaged in subsistence farming or any variety of work in urban areas, the situation is the same.

In paid work outside the home, women lose out on all scores. They are at a disadvantage in the job market because of lower education and training levels, cultural prejudice and domestic responsibilities. They are the most underpaid, the most under-employed, the most unskilled and the least organized in trade unions. But the major and over-riding problem, for men and women alike, is unemployment: in El Salvador there is no social security system for the unemployed.

Half the male population is economically active, compared to one-quarter of the female population. Women are most heavily concentrated in the sales and service sectors, accounting for some 60% to 70% of the work-force, generally speaking the worst paid areas of work. In agriculture and related activities, women only make up 18.2% of the total workforce, but this is a vast under-estimate because of inadequate census categories.[1]

Women's Work in Rural Areas

Subsistence farming remains the main form of economic activity but the problems of insufficient or inadequate lands, heavy indebtedness and lack of credits have made it more and more difficult for families to survive by farming alone. Both men and women must also look for paid work and many have been forced to migrate into the cities. For those who remain in the country, life is very arduous:

You get up at 4.00 a.m., that's the way with work in the country. First you light the fire, then make the coffee and fetch water from the well. Our nearest well was some 30 minutes away so that was an hour walking in all. I had to make several trips every day, carrying one bucket on my head and another resting on my hip. The children would help with some of the trips.

Then you have to wash, grind and pat the maize for the tortillas. If you're quick, you can grind all the maize in about two hours. I would prepare about 60 tortillas every day because that was all we had to eat – tortillas and beans. We rarely had anything else. We rented a plot of land and so I would have to take the meal out to my husband at mid-day. That was some hour and a half away. In the afternoon, I would stay and help with work. We grew maize, millet and beans.

At 6 p.m. we would return home. Then I'd prepare the next meal; sometimes we would have rice as well as beans. We went to bed about 8 p.m. We didn't have electricity only candles and paraffin. That's why there are so many children – no television!

I'd usually leave the washing until Sunday, also the sewing and mending. They say Sunday is a day of rest, but there's no rest for the poor; every day is a work day.

Yolanda, San Salvador, April 1983

There are few women agricultural workers, although some wives and daughters cook or do other domestic tasks on the big estates. Prior to 1965, women were employed more frequently, usually as part of a family unit, but when the Rivera regime (1962–7) brought in a minimum wage

Table 2.1   Women s Participation in Employment According to Sector

	Sector	Total	%	Female	%Female
1.	Agriculture, hunting forestry & fishing	636,617	40.0	115,918	18.2
2.	Mining & quarrying	4,394	0.2	291	6.2
3.	Manufacturing	247,621	15.6	103,506	41.8
4.	Electr., gas & water	9,681	0.6	853	8.8
5.	Construction	80,089	5.0	352	0.4
6.	Wholesale/retail trade restaurants & hotels	256,086	16.1	177,301	69.2
7.	Transport, storage & communications	65,593	4.1	2,599	3.9
8.	Financing, insur., real estate, etc.	15,863	1.0	5,433	34.2
9.	Community, social & personal services	250,158	15.7	129,013	51.5
10.	Not adequately defined	224	—	112	—
11.	Persons seeking their first job	27,027	1.7	18,529	68.5
Total		1,593,353	100.0	553,907	34.7

Source: *International Labour Office*, 1982

for permanent agricultural workers, many estate owners stopped hiring women.

For the purpose of wage assessment in rural areas, women are bracketed with minors and the partially handicapped, demonstrating a clear cultural prejudice at an official level. Women earn some 20% less than men.[2]

Women mainly work as seasonal workers in the most labour-intensive and least mechanized jobs in the harvesting of the three main export crops: coffee, cotton and sugar. Harvesting is a delicate task requiring deft fingers and precision, for which women are supposed by nature to be peculiarly suited. In fact, it is an acquired skill, although not recognized as such, nor paid accordingly. Workers are usually paid on a piece-work system and receive no legal or social benefits as they are not applicable to temporary agricultural work.

Labour Code for Temporary Agricultural Workers

The political importance of the landed oligarchy is clearly reflected in the Salvadorean Labour Code. Legal provisions for temporary agricultural workers are minimal:

Art. 87: Temporary agricultural workers do not possess the right to stability in their work and consequently, either party can terminate the contract at any time, without giving due cause and without any responsibility.

Art. 89: Workers who give their services in harvests may work in excess of the limits of the ordinary working day; work fulfilled in excess of the ordinary working day will be remunerated with the equivalent of payment for the ordinary salary. Also, workers may work for two consecutive weeks, substituting the day of rest of the first week for the Saturday of the second week, hence enjoying two consecutive days of rest; but work fulfilled on the substituted Sunday will be remunerated only with the payment for an ordinary working day.

A survey carried out in 1978–9, during the harvest season between October and March, found that almost 30% of all Salvadorean households were engaged in harvest work. They earned an average weekly wage of 47 colones (US$18.8): 39% of the workforce were women, and 14% of females and 16% of males were below the age of 15.[3]

Both in coffee-and cotton-harvesting, women are subjected to enormous health hazards. In coffee-harvesting, women carry a basket on their front, which when full weighs up to 5 kilos. Although there are no studies for El Salvador, research in Mexico shows that the weight of the basket can cause damage to the spinal column, so that it becomes slightly twisted and exerts pressure on the uterus. As a consequence, abnormally high rates of spontaneous abortions among women coffee-harvesters have been recorded.[4] In cotton-harvesting, the use of pesticides has provoked severe or fatal cases of poisoning. According to a report by the Central American Institute of Research and Industrial Technology, Salvadoreans living in the cotton-producing areas suffered from levels of DDT in the body 11 times higher than the corresponding average found in Florida, USA.[5] Despite a very elaborate legal code on the use of pesticides, introduced in 1973, the situation remains unchanged.

A campesina woman described her annual odyssey in search of any type of agricultural work:

> At the age of 16, I started to work in all kinds of crop harvesting, coffee, maize and sugarcane. I lived in the Department of Sonsonate but we went all over the place looking for work. Almost all our village would go – brothers, sisters, relatives and friends, arriving home every fortnight, unless we had the good fortune to be working nearby.
>
> We'd pick coffee from October to January, but January is called the stagnant month. We would glean the last of the coffee but hardly got paid anything. You had to search through half the estate to gather a pound of coffee for 2 colones. Or we would go to the coast to pick cotton, which is really exhausting. The fields there are a source of a lot of sickness, particularly with the pollution. The poisons they use in the fields are very strong and we're always having to take people off to the hospital. They'd give you two and a half sacks as a quota for every day and if you didn't manage it, they didn't pay you anything. Men have always been paid 5 colones more than women or children and we all do exactly the same work. When the rains come in May, there's work sowing maize, fertilizing the coffee plants or making irrigation ditches; you do this until October when you start with the coffee crop again.
>
> I wanted to find a better job, but for a factory you need to have finished school and in the coffee processing industries they ask for ninth grade. On the estates, they don't make so many demands, but even there, it's not easy to find work. I have been living in the city for three years and if I were to go to the estates now they wouldn't give me work. In 1979, they were hiring less people, giving jobs to men rather than women. Things are much worse now.
> San Salvador, April 1983

In rural areas, despite soaring inflation, wages have been frozen by government decree since 1979 and have dropped in real terms by 69.3% between 1971–81.[6]

It is increasingly difficult to survive in the countryside and women's daily lives are filled with devastating insecurity. Campesinos are hard hit by the economic crisis and government forces have deliberately destroyed the livelihood of many subsistence farming families.

Table 2.2   Women's Wages as a % of Men's Wages in the
Manufacturing Industry

	1979		1980	
	San Salvador	Other Areas	San Salvador	Other Areas
All industries	76%	65%	61%	89%
Clothing, textiles	86%	81%	83%	96%
Food, drink, tobacco	81%	82%	81%	83%

Source: MINIPLAN, *Indicadores Económicos y Sociales*, 1981

Women in Industry

Women make up just over 40% of the industrial workforce. They work predominantly in industries such as food-processing, clothing and textiles and in the multinational assembly plants in the industrial free zones.[7]

At best, working conditions in manufacturing are very poor, but women are always the worst off. Wages average approximately 7 to 12 times less than the corresponding rates in the USA.[8] One third of the male workforce, but only one-tenth of the female workforce, earn above the minimum salary.[9] Over three-quarters of all women are classed as unskilled or semi-skilled, compared to under two-thirds of all men.[10] In 1980, women earned on average 81% of men's wages in manufacturing.[11]

The Labour Code prohibits unequal pay on the grounds of sex in urban areas but no known case has ever been brought against discriminatory pay practices. Women are bracketed with minors and the code is basically concerned with the protection of women as the 'weaker sex'. While it includes a very extensive list of dangerous or insalubrious work conditions for women, the two specific demands of women workers, equal pay for equal work and the provision of nursery facilities, do not receive the same emphasis. In the Labour Code, no legal obligation to provide nursery facilities has been included and only in recent years has a clause been added to the effect that the state *will* regulate the obligation of employers to maintain nurseries (Art. 183).

Paula worked for seven years in a biscuit factory in San Salvador, owned jointly by a Czech and a Salvadorean. The factory, *Productos Alimenticios Diana S.A.*, employed 1,500 workers, 75% women. The departments which employed men were paid above the minimum wage and men's jobs were invariably classified as more skilled activities. Paula entered the factory at the age of 17 after finishing secondary school and found that her wage was so low, she was forced to work exceptionally long hours, from 7.30 a.m. to 9.30 p.m. The majority of women workers were between 20 and 25 as the management felt they had fewer problems with young women. The factory also illegally employed children, normally the sons and daughters of employees who found that their own wages were insufficient. Despite the size of the factory, there were no nursery facilities and mothers were sometimes forced to bring in their young children and leave them in the cloakrooms all day.

> There were many departments where the work was very heavy. In the sections where maize and bananas were cooked, we worked in front of a blazing open fire all day long. The ventilation was very bad too. Many contracted lung diseases, rheumatism and allergies from the acidic ingredients they touched. The noise levels were deafening and you came off work feeling your head would explode. There were dangerous jobs and little in the way of safety precautions. One woman had her finger cut off in a slicing machine and never received any compensation. Or rather, her only compensation was receiving the sack.
>
> The supervisors constantly bothered the women, making insulting remarks and insinuating things. In many cases, in order to obtain a loan, the women would have to go to bed with one of the supervisors or the boss.
> Mexico, May 1982

Cecilia works in a small coffee factory in Ilopango which employs 118 women out of a total of 280 employees. The women work exclusively in the packing department, putting coffee into different size packets. It is the worst paid department of the entire factory:

> I was earning 4 colones a day when the cost of a kilo of meat was between 2 or 3 colones. Now, because of the decree laws, the situation is worse. Salary increases over 10% are forbidden. In 1981 the government declared a 10% increase in those factories where it was economically viable, but we only received a 5% rise and our factory was very well off in economic terms. After the nationalization of the coffee industry in 1979, the company made a good deal with INCAFE, the state marketing board. They had no problem with the supply of raw materials and their market was guaranteed by the government. In 1982, we were given another 5% rise although inflation was well over 50%. Since then we have had no more increases. We earn 300 colones a fortnight and my husband, two children and I spend 150 colones on food alone. We can only afford to eat meat twice a week, the rest of the time it's beans and rice. The rent for our house, which only has two small rooms, is 250 colones. Since the elections, our situation has become even worse. There's no longer money to buy clothes. A pair of trousers now costs 95 colones.
> San Salvador, April 1983

Since 1979, the economic crisis has devastated employment opportunities; following the world-wide pattern, women have been the first to lose their jobs. The multinationals have moved to other countries because of the civil war and according to the last report, in May 1983, there were only four factories still operating in the multinational industrial parks. Between 1979–81, an estimated 330 industries closed down, leaving 22,439 people out of work.[12] Per capita consumer expenditure as a consequence had reached early 1960s levels at the end of 1982.

The Informal Sector

As unemployment has risen, more and more women have been forced to invent work for themselves in the informal sector, in street sales or occasional domestic work. Two-thirds of the urban female workforce are engaged in commerce and services,[13] the two main categories which cover the informal sector. They are also the two categories of work where earnings are most frequently below the 'poverty line'.[14]

Informal sector activities include such occupations as street-vending of lottery tickets, food, combs, cigarettes and the inevitable chewing gum. It also includes women who engage in occasional washing or cleaning. Migrant campesina women can rarely expect to find jobs other than in domestic service or the informal sector, although, of course, for all women, the oldest profession – prostitution – offers an alternative to unemployment.

Domestic Workers

> The situation of women is terrible . . . But, women have a better chance in San Salvador, because you can work with the rich, while men can't do that. It's easier for women to get work.
> Domestic worker, San Salvador, April 1983

In 1980, 13.6% of the total female workforce was engaged in domestic work, amounting to a total of some 60,000 women. Over 95% of all domestic workers were female.[15]

The majority of domestic workers are young women without any formal education who have come in from the countryside. They either live in or are 'dailies'. Those who live in normally receive room and board plus a wage – often well below the legal minimum. They work six days a week or more, on no fixed terms, with no formal protection and are expected to be available all day long including late into the evening. Three-quarters of all domestic workers work more than 60 hours a week.[16] Young and far from home, they suffer from emotional deprivation and severe isolation. Their middle-class employers are suspicious and often accuse them of petty theft and idleness. They can be subjected to verbal and physical abuse and sexual harassment is all too common. They either share the children's room or are given 'quarters', normally small, box-like rooms either on the roof or behind the kitchen.

Labour Code for Domestic Servants

The Labour Code is exceptionally vague when it comes to work contracts, pay and conditions for domestic workers and reflects a series of prejudices. Compliance with its provisions is virtually non-existent and most domestic workers have no knowledge of it.

Art. 76: The work contract for domestic service may be arranged verbally. If this is the case, the employer is obliged to provide, at the petition of the worker, every 30 days, a written confirmation of employment, which may be written on ordinary writing paper and signed by the employer. It should state the name and surname of both parties, the period of service, salary received in the last month and the place and date of the document's emission.

Art. 80: A worker in domestic service is not subjected to any particular working schedule, but should enjoy a daily period of rest of at least 12 hours, of which 10 must be consecutive and during the night; and the other two hours should be assigned to meal periods; in addition a paid day of rest should be allocated every week, which may be accumulated up to a number of 3 days.

Art. 81: A worker in domestic service is obliged to give his/her services on official holidays when asked to do so by the employer. In such a case, the worker may claim the right to an additional 100% of the daily salary for work carried out during these days.

Non-residents are, as a rule, women with children and therefore not acceptable for living-in posts. They earn slightly higher wages – but again, often below the legal minimum – and lack any job security or social security benefits.

Domestic work provides an important source of income for a campesino family and the earnings of many domestic workers are sent home. One woman explained that before she was married, she would be sent into the capital city to look for domestic work when the harvest had been poor or some additional expense, such as medicine or a funeral, had to be covered. But domestic work was unjust and humiliating:

They ask you for every kind of documentation you can imagine and then treat you like some kind of being that is half-human, half-dog, who doesn't have any private life of her own. If you haven't got your medical certificate, your letter of recommendation, your proof of no record with the police, your identity card – no job. And many of us don't know how to read and write and every government document costs money. And even so, they treat you as a likely criminal. One family gave me a day off every month, told me I had to be back before nine in the evening and checked my bag when I left to see if I hadn't robbed anything. The kind of treatment you have to put up with is disgraceful and if you don't, you simply get fired. And that's the worst, not having a job, nowhere to go and nowhere to live. But now I think that the Nicaraguan women are an example to us. They have learnt to organize, taken up arms and have fought for the right to be treated like human beings and that's what we're doing now.

Domestic worker and member of the Committee of Mothers, Mexico City, September 1982

Prostitution

Prostitution is widespread, an integral part of a highly poverty-ridden and *machista* society, where it is common for adolescent boys to be taken by relatives to a brothel for their sexual initiation. In addition, a large migrant labour force is conducive to prostitution. In San Salvador there are two notorious districts. A nearby beach resort (Majahuál) is famous for its gambling and prostitution facilities.

The state has managed both to condone and to condemn prostitution. Many members of the oligarchy, particularly the military, have powerful financial interests in gambling and prostitution, but on the other hand, prostitutes are always in danger of finding themselves outside the margin of the law.

In the 1950s, the government of Colonel Oscar Osorio (1950–6) passed a law prohibiting prostitution in El Salvador, although it had little effect beyond filling the prisons for a short time. Salvador Cayetano Carpio, writing in 1954, described the prostitutes in the prison where he was being clandestinely held:

Chinona, Julia and Rosa Candida are almost permanent guests of the prison. They spend their days shouting and screaming in the cell, and then they are finally let out. But the following afternoon, one of them is brought back, drunk, shrieking, insulting everyone in sight. A few days later, they're all back together again, showing off their syphilitic bodies through the bars of the cell, raucously singing the latest juke box hits . . .

The authorities, protectors of public morality, make categorical declarations in the press, stating that they are determined to put an end to vice and prostitution. As a result of raids on the taverns and cheaper brothels (the high class brothels are not touched as they belong to the military), the small women's cell becomes absolutely packed. And the more crowded, the more satisfied the police, as that means they are efficiently carrying out the law against prostitution – one of the present government's most notable social 'contributions'. It is also one of their plans to put an end to the 'danger of communism' through combating these social blights. To eliminate the problems of prostitution, they sometimes take the women from the cell, put them in an ambulance and drive them over the border to Honduras.[17]

21

Today the situation has not changed fundamentally. The vast majority of 'common criminals', as opposed to the political prisoners in the Women's Prison, are prostitutes serving a six-month sentence for working without a licence. Although the prison is euphemistically called a rehabilitation centre, the women staff workers are known to arrange appointments for the prostitutes with the male guards in exchange for a small return and there is no attempt to train the women to help them find some other form of employment when they are freed.

The Salvadorean left has consistently condemned prostitution. Some of the popular organizations have begun to work with prostitutes, though they admit that it is a very difficult task. A member of the FDR talked about prostitutes in Santa Ana, a provincial capital in one of the main coffee-growing regions of El Salvador:

In Santa Ana, prostitution is organized by the military and it is a very lucrative business. Many brothels are almost entirely for their use. Women turn to prostitution at a very early age, 14 or even younger. The youngest and the prettiest are naturally for the exclusive use of the bourgeoisie. They live in brothels with gambling facilities as well. Each brothel has to obtain a special licence from the police and the names of the women must also be registered. The women must undergo monthly medical check-ups. If all the women are not registered, the police may make a raid on the brothel, taking the unregistered women to prison until the owner of the brothel pays a fine. They do not receive a fixed income, but have board and lodgings free. They are regarded as the elite amongst the prostitutes.

Others gather in Parque Colón in the centre of the city to solicit. They are known as the 'listed women' as they are also registered with the police. Compared to the brothel prostitutes, they are dowdy and unkempt and they have a lot more problems with the police. They are frequently hauled off to prison and treated very badly, beaten and insulted, at times, even raped. These women tend to be fairly rough and uncouth, and their clientele are mainly from the criminal underworld – thieves, drug-dealers, heavy drinkers.

And finally, there are the so-called 'occasional prostitutes'. Many of these are women who work during the day and solicit at night in order to earn a bit more money.

In Santa Ana, the army held a 'moral clean-up' campaign. They murdered many criminals and prostitutes. It was a decoy to hide the fact that they were also killing members of the political opposition. Other prostitutes were killed because they had shown some sympathy towards the organizations. I knew 'Chilindrina', who was only 17 or 18 when she was murdered. It seems that at a Sunday dance at the 'El Greco' Bar, she expressed some sympathy towards the revolutionary movement and somebody overheard her. She was raped and then killed and a few days later her naked corpse found somewhere in the hills.

There are many prostitutes who now collaborate with the revolutionary organizations. Others have given up prostitution and joined an organization full-time, like one 19-year-old I worked with. In Santa Ana, she couldn't do political work because of her bad reputation, so she left her child with her mother and joined the mass organization in San Salvador. Recently I heard she feels a lot better doing something for her country.

The problem of prostitution will have to be one of the priorities of the FDR–FMLN after they take power. With training and new work possibilities, I believe we will gradually be able to improve their situation.

Alicia, Mexico City, June 1983

Notes

1. See C. Wainerman and Z. Recchini de Lattes, *El trabajo femenino en el banquillo de los acusados: La medición censal en América Latina* (Terra Nova, Mexico, 1981), for a good critique of census categories.

2. Male agricultural workers received 5.20 colones per day and women agricultural workers 4.60 colones per day in June 1981. *Indicadores económicos y sociales, julio–diciembre 1981* (Ministerio de Planificación y Coordinación del Desarrollo Económico y Social, San Salvador, September 1982).

3. *Encuesta sobre movilidad temporal de los trabajadores en época de cosecha de café, algodón y caña de azucar, octubre 1978–abril 1979* (Ministerio de Planificación y Coordinación del Desarrollo Económico y Social – Unidad de Investigaciones Muestrales).

4. Cecilia Sheridan Prieto, *Mujer obrera y organización social: El sindicato de obreras desmanchadoras de café, Coatepec, Veracruz: Un estudio histórico-monográfico*, Cuadernos de la Casa Chata, No. 76 (Centro de Investigaciones y Estudios Superiores en Antropología Social, Mexico, D.F., 1983), and interview with author in Mexico, May 1982.

5. *Salud en El Salvador – Otra razón para el combate popular* (AGEUS, Costa Rica, 1981), note 2, p. 37.

6. Real minimum wages have dropped by 52% from 1971–81 and in agricultural work by 69.3%. *Boletín de Ciencias Económicas y Sociales* (Universidad Centroamericana 'José Simeón Cañas', El Salvador, Año V, Nov.–Dec. 1982), nos. 54–5, p. 379.

7. The concentration of women in industry is highest in the clothing and textile industries (70% and 36.8%, respectively). *Agricultural Sector Assessment: El Salvador* (United States Agency for International Development, Washington D.C., 1977), p. 28.

8. 'International Subcontracting Arrangements in Electronics Between Developed Market Economy Countries and Developing Countries', UNCTAD, New York, TD/B/C.2/144, Supp. 1, 1975, pp. 20–1.

9. *Encuesta de hogares de propósitos multiples (II) 1978* (MINIPLAN, El Salvador).

10. *Encuesta de formación profesional 1978* (MINIPLAN, El Salvador).

11. *Indicadores económicos y sociales*.

12. *Boletín de ciencias económicas y sociales*, p. 380.

13. 66.4% of the total female workforce are engaged in services and commerce (51% in services and 70% in commerce according to government figures). *Indicadores económicos y sociales*.

14. World Bank, *El Salvador: An Inquiry into Urban Poverty* (Washington, USA, April 1980), p. 9.

15. *Indicadores económicos y sociales*.

16. *El Salvador: An Inquiry into Urban Poverty*.

17. Salvador Cayetano Carpio, *Secuestro y Capucha* (EDUCA, Costa Rica, 1979), pp. 194–5.

3 Women's Health

We don't go to the hospital. At the Santa Ana hospital, they treat you like animals. Most people don't bother to go.
Campesina woman from Santa Ana, San Salvador, April 1983

The health conditions of the vast majority of Salvadoreans can only be described as critical and it is women who must bear the brunt of caring for the ill.

General indices of health are among the worst in the world, ranking with such countries as Bangladesh and Haiti. El Salvador has the lowest per capita calorie intake in Latin America, and preventable gastric diseases combined with malnutrition are the most common cause of death. While life expectancy has risen from 46 years in 1961 to 59 years in 1977, 20% of the infant population still die before reaching the age of five.

In 1977, only 45% of the population had access to public health services and 9% to the private sector.[1] The Ministry of Public Health effectively covered only some 30% of the population; the other 15% able to make use of public health services were covered by health insurance through the workplace.

All medical facilities have been heavily concentrated in the capital city. The metropolitan area possessed 50% of all hospital beds and 70% of all qualified doctors in 1979, although only 16% of the total population were living in the capital.[2] There is an acute shortage of medical personnel – only one doctor per 3,700 inhabitants and one trained nurse per 4,000 inhabitants in 1977.[3]

Most public health service doctors work in more than one job and, because pay and conditions are so poor, many doctors and nurses decide to leave El Salvador. In 1979, it was estimated that some 24.8% of all qualified doctors were living abroad.[4]

In common with most Third World countries, the pharmaceutical industry is in the hands of multinational companies and there is no effective quality control over their products. There is a government Sanitary Committee, but doctors report members as corrupt and irresponsible and companies operating their own control mechanisms can afford to be very lax. Multinationals are not obliged to provide detailed information about products and in practice there are no restrictions on buying any product over the chemist counter without prescription.

Over the last three years, the health services and general levels of health have deteriorated significantly. In 1983, public health and social welfare received one of the biggest expenditure cuts of all the public sectors. Declared expenditure on defence and security is now more than double the expenditure on health. Medicine and money from the public health budget are being unofficially transferred to the military health services and at least five regional hospitals and a number of smaller health centres have been taken over for use by the military.

A trained nurse, now forced into exile in Mexico City, had worked in the Maternity Hospital of San Salvador until 1981 and described conditions there:

> After the coup, a military doctor, Col. Dr Tomás Calvo, was put in charge of the hospital, the budget was reduced and unofficially, much of the hospital finances and medicines were transferred to the military services. In 1981, when I left, there was no surgical alcohol available and we had to make do with boiled water. The patients were being given yucca roots and chayote fruits as the main meal of the day and there was no milk available for the babies. As many women are anaemic and unable to breast-feed, most babies were affected. There was a shortage of beds and women had to share. Cleaning staff had been drastically cut and we often couldn't find a change of sheets after a delivery.
>
> The situation wasn't so bad before. There were medicines, vitamins and a balanced diet for the mothers. There was always a long wait for an appointment, sometimes up to a month, and women were only kept in for 24 hours if it was a normal birth. Now, with this new director, everything is going to the army barracks. What's happening in that hospital is nothing short of a crime.
> Elisa, Mexico City, September 1982

Official health statistics bear less and less resemblance to the truth. Since 1979, the Ministry of Public Health and Social Welfare statistics have shown a miraculous improvement after decades of progressive deterioration. Maternal, infant and child mortality have all decreased, according to the last report published for 1981.[5] However, a US medical team visiting El Salvador in January 1982 reported a 'virtually complete breakdown in the health system'. They stated that basic equipment and medicines were in short supply and that antibiotics and analgesics were particularly scarce. Conditions in rural areas were described as 'devastating':

> In some rural areas, infant mortality affects two out of three children. 40% of children are born with body weights less than 2.5 kilos or 5.5 pounds. One third of the population is clinically anaemic and 80% of children under 5 years of age suffer from malnutrition.[6]

Maternal Health

Maternity is a dangerous period for women and figures for perinatal mortality, natural and induced abortions with serious complications and still-births are very high. Maternal mortality is five times higher in El Salvador than in the US. Perinatal mortality is the seventh most common cause of death and only one-third of all deliveries or miscarriages received medical attention in 1975.[7]

A small survey among campesina women living in the eastern part of the country, one of the poorest areas, suggested that women live in a state verging on terror during pregnancy, fearing death, or at least a permanent decline in their general level of health. 40% of the women interviewed considered pregnancy should be treated as a disease and 87% thought that the perinatal period was a 'highly dangerous' time for them.[8]

Induced Abortions

Induced abortion, as in all Latin American countries, is illegal. The Penal Code of 1977 only allows abortions on health grounds or because of pregnancies as a result of rape. Penalties for induced abortions are fierce in theory but ineffective in practice. Doctors who are known to carry out abortions merely pay off the necessary authorities and are rarely persecuted. There are two known 'clandestine' abortion clinics in San Salvador which provide an expensive but hygienic service for the rich. However, for the great majority, such services are beyond their reach. A gynaecologist who worked in the Maternity Hospital in San Salvador saw at least five women every day who were suffering from serious complications after a badly performed abortion. Approximately one-third of all beds in gynaecological wards are taken up by women in the same condition.[9]

Statistics do not distinguish between induced and spontaneous abortions. However, the 1978 Contraceptive Prevalence Survey recognized induced abortion as a 'public health problem' and the World Bank has termed it 'the most common form of birth control' in El Salvador

The FDR–FMLN has made no statement on abortion and there are few who would advocate making induced abortions legal or part of health service provisions. The Maternity Hospital gynaecologist was a young doctor in his twenties and his work had brought him constantly up against this problem. He believed that induced abortion was an 'outrage against women's health when performed in inadequate conditions' but he did not believe that it should be made legal.

Popular Medicine and Healing

In rural areas, modern medicine is sometimes rejected on the grounds that it is intrinsically bad. For others, a visit to the clinic may involve a long journey, time lost and money spent, with the net result a prescription for medicine which there is no possibility of buying. Herbal remedies therefore still remain very important and it is campesina women rather than men who know about the healing properties of local herbs and pass their knowledge down from one generation to the next.

> There are a lot of herbs for when a child falls ill. Our most frequent illnesses are stomach problems, like diarrhoea and vomiting. Here we use *guano* for stomach problems, or an *horchata de guineo tierno* or an *horchata de guayaba*. For diarrhoea, you can use *horchata de pochata de huerta* and for vomiting, *yerba buena*.
> Campesina woman, San Salvador, April 1983

In the towns, markets contain whole sections given over to stalls with a vast variety of herbs and roots for every conceivable ailment from toothache to tuberculosis.

Most rural communities support a local midwife who may also be a *curandera* or healer. Although they have received no professional training, they have learnt from the older generations a huge wealth of practical knowledge about childbirth and provide an invaluable service to the community. They are greatly respected women within their community.

Niña Santos (Niña means 'child' in Spanish) was an old lady in her sixties, the midwife of a small farming community of some 1,000 inhabitants in the department of La Libertad, some 75 km outside of San Salvador, 30 minutes walk from the main road and with no electricity or running water. Her house was made of bamboo poles and straw:

> I do this only because there isn't perhaps anybody else. I don't have any formal training. If I know something, it's because the Lord has given me some understanding. I do it because in these hills, being poor, one feels responsible and many people can't afford the trip to the nearest town. I acquired the skills to do this before I knew about the world, purely because of God's will. I began at the age of 16, and now I'm over 60. I've lost count of how many women I have helped.
> They come to me to ask for advice, to see if the child is all right, or to check when it is due. You can feel how the child is positioned with your hands and if it's not well, I turn it round until it's in the right position. I don't give them medicine from chemists. I use lime roots and other herbs like *chinamiotle* which has the same results. I boil it like a tea and it helps hurry the process up, if the woman is ready.
> I have had difficult cases, like the woman who had been given a Caesarean operation: giving birth after that kind of operation is very delicate, but it

turned out all right. Some come before they're due because there's an eclipse of the sun or the moon. There are also problems when the moon shines on a pregnant woman through a crack. The moon eats the child's mouth, nose or the part which is exposed. Other difficulties occur when the woman doesn't have what she feels like eating and the child suffers. In these cases, you can give them a bit of salt, or an acidic herb which calms the child while you look for what the woman craves, like butter or fruit. I've had difficult cases, that's true, but no mother has ever died. I've delivered two still-born babies, but no one has ever died in my hands.
La Libertad, April 1983

There has been no serious study of the persistence of Indian beliefs about the origins of diseases or supernatural cures since a study in 1957,[10] but they are still current among the older generation at least. While perhaps belief in spiritual forces is becoming less widespread, herbal remedies, *curanderas* and self-trained midwives continue to be of vital importance to the rural and urban poor. Experience of the present Salvadorean health services and economic restrictions on buying Western medicine are reinforcing this knowledge, not eroding it.

Notes

1. *Situación y perspectivas del empleo en El Salvador*, PREALC, International Labour Office, Santiago, Chile, 1977, pp. 82–3.
2. World Bank Studies, op. cit., p. 27.
3. Ibid.
4. *Salud en El Salvador*, p. 85.
5. *Indicadores Económicos y Sociales, Julio–Diciembre 1981*.
6. *Report of the Public Health Delegation of Inquiry* (Committee for Health Rights in El Salvador, New York, January 1983).
7. *Salud en El Salvador*, p. 21.
8. Polly Harrison, 'La campesina y su salud mental: el caso salvadoreño', paper presented at the first Mexican-Central American Symposium of Research on Women, 7–8 November (Colegio de México, D.F., 1977).
9. T. Monreal *et al.*, 'Abortos hospitalizados en El Salvador', *Salud Pública en México*, Epoca 5, vol. XIX, no. 3 (May–June 1977), pp. 387–95.
10. Richard N. Adams, *Cultural Studies of Panama, Nicaragua, Guatemala, El Salvador, Honduras* (Pan American Sanitary Bureau, World Health Organization, 1957, republished by Blaire Ethridge, Detroit, USA, 1976).

4 Family Relations

Family relations continue to be very important both economically and socially in El Salvador. For the poor, the family network represents a crucial welfare system and for the rich, access to political power is determined by family ties and influence. The Salvadorean oligarchy is still a closed circle of families which over generations have inter-married to maintain their wealth and privilege within their own small group.

For women, the family and 'motherhood' is the central focus of their lives and a childless woman is regarded as an aberration, sometimes almost a social outcast. Most women must live in open contradiction with their own moral code, for while they regard marriage as a fundamental aim in life, El Salvador has one of the lowest marriage rates in the hemisphere. Civil and religious marriages tend to be the prerogative of the elite, a reflection of the precarious economic situation of the majority of the population. Both men and women must migrate in search of work and there is little need to secure inheritance through marriage.

The Civil Code

The Civil Code affects only a minority of women. While it has been revised in recent years and women do have *patria potestad* or legal rights over their children, whether legitimate or not, some clauses of the code still remain exceptionally antiquated and reflect male privilege. Adultery is a criminal offence:

Art. 265, Penal Code:
Prison sentences of six months to two years will be passed on:
1. A married woman who has had carnal access to any man other than her husband and the man if he does so in the knowledge that she is married.
2. A married man who keeps a concubine in contempt of his wife or good customs or who fails to meet his obligations to maintain his family.

While women must not be unfaithful, men must not make a scandal of their affairs. An accepted practice among rich men is to support two houses, the official residence with wife and children and the mistress, probably also with children, in the renowned *casa chica* or little house.

Divorce by mutual consent was introduced as early as 1902, but even today it is by no means socially acceptable, particularly among the upper classes where the family remains 'sacred'.

Extended families living in the same household remain very common. In a study of the slum areas of San Salvador in 1978, one-fifth of households were 'co-residential kinship groups with no regularly present male in the role of husband or father' and 10% of households were formed by multiple or extended families.[1]

It is not uncommon for women to have children by several different fathers and men may often be loosely attached to a number of households at the same time. Particularly among the urban poor, there is a phenomenally high number of single mothers.[2] Men are notoriously 'macho' and have few scruples about abandoning their women, who are left to take sole responsibility for their children.

Table 4.1   Marital Status of Salvadorean Women

	San Salvador (%)	Rural Areas (%)
Married	26.0	30.8
Free-unions	26.7	32.5
Single	30.1	29.9
Divorced/widowed	17.2	13.8

Source: FESAL survey, 1978

The civil war has aggravated this situation, causing a breakdown in family life, such as it was. Both men and women have left home to join political or military organizations and families have been separated by death, imprisonment or enforced exile. Among the refugee communities, new forms of collective living arrangements have been organized. Many women have permanently or temporarily adopted children from other families and are establishing community child-care facilities.

Family Welfare

The Salvadorean government has no family welfare programmes although, according to the Constitution, the family 'should be specially protected by the State'. There are a variety of voluntary social welfare organizations run by philanthropic wives with time on their hands but these organizations receive no state funding. Women politicians and government ministers are prone to remark that the family is the foundation-stone of society and should be strengthened but at the same time realize, as Dra. Julia Castillo, Vice-President of the Constituent Assembly remarked: 'The majority of Salvadorean women have not been supported by marriage and they must make enormous sacrifices' (San Salvador, April 1983). The only government department which assists women and children is the Family Relations Department of the Advocate General of the Poor (*Procuraduría General de los Pobres, PGP*), which provides legal aid for women who wish to get child maintenance through the courts from the father. The system is peculiarly ineffective as the father must first voluntarily recognize paternity and the PGP can only enforce payments by docking money from the father's salary if he is in steady employment in an urban area. The state itself provides no financial assistance whatsoever to mothers in need. Dra. Dina Castro, Advocate General of the Poor, also recognized that the situation of single mothers was 'critical', although her government department was doing nothing to assist them.

Equally, the state is obliged in theory to protect children at risk. A few children's homes have been opened but they also double as reformatories for young offenders. The *Centro de Orientación Rosa Virginia Pelletier* is under armed guard and is run to all intents and purposes as if it were a prison, although in 1980 there were only two young offenders in residence. The other 150 girls were children at risk or those who had been abandoned.[3]

Sexual Oppression

Salvadorean women often remark that they live in a 'matriarchal society', by which they mean they must support their children single-handed. In fact, authoritarian patriarchal relations between the sexes are all too prevalent. The socially sanctioned dominance of male over female has hardly been questioned in Salvadorean society and domestic violence and sexual assault are largely unrecognized and go unreported:

> Wife-beating is very common, almost accepted as natural. Where I worked in the university, if a woman came in covered in bruises, no one would say anything, although we all knew what had happened. Rape is an equally taboo subject. There must be thousands of cases of rape or child-abuse – apart from what the security forces are up to – but again they never get talked about. I doubt whether a girl would dare tell her parents, let alone take the matter to court.
> Eva, Mexico City, June 1983

There is still enormous importance attached to virginity and girls are consequently protected, or beaten into submission, and their social activities greatly restricted. In rural areas, it is common for fathers to 'marry off' their daughters, whether formally or informally, shortly after puberty.

Indigenous Marriages

There are very few self-identifying indigenous communities left in El Salvador, unlike its neighbour Guatemala. In El Salvador, they represent under 5% of the population and in Guatemala, some 70%. The 1932 campesino uprising was identified by the military in government as an 'Indian revolt' and entire indigenous communities were slaughtered, an estimated 30,000 people. The survivors, fearing further reprisals, abandoned their native customs and tried to blend with the *mestizo* populations. The communities that exist today – of Mayan and Nahuatl descent – are the Pipiles, the Nonualcos, the Izalcos and the Lencas but they have lost nearly all their customs, including language, dress and political and religious traditions. This account of an Indian marriage, still practised some 60 years ago, is just an indication of the existence of a cultural system which was destroyed by the Salvadorean oligarchy and military.

> Each different indigenous group has its own marriage customs and ceremonies . . . Once the Panchos have agreed to a wedding, the parents of the young man send a live chicken to the betrothed. Then follows a bitter night for the girl. Her parents try and make her confess to any past misdemeanours with another man. It is customary to give the girl a good beating to make her tell the truth. Then the chicken is prepared. If the girl has confessed to anything, the chicken is seasoned but instead of crossing the legs inside the body, they are left splayed on the outside. When the chicken is returned in this way, the wedding is cancelled and the girl's parents return all the gifts.
>
> But when the girl is worthy of the honour of being married, the chicken is returned as it should be: with the legs crossed and put inside the body. As soon as the parents of the young man receive the chicken, they visit the future wife, taking her a rosary and necklace which she will wear on the wedding day.
>
> Maria de Baratta, *Cuscatlán Típico* (Ministerio de Cultura, San Salvador, 1950), p. 320

It has been suggested that in some rural areas, cliteridectomy is practised,[4] but there have been no confirmed reports and it would seem unlikely as it was not a characteristic of Meso-american cultures. It is certainly not a widespread or systematic custom, nor is genital mutilation a 'marriage requirement' as is the case in some African or Middle Eastern societies. However, it is undoubtedly true that sexual abuse of children and young girls is very widespread. Many local *caciques* or large landowners expect to have sexual access to campesina women, particularly young girls, living on or near their estates. Class relations are such that it would be very difficult for a campesino family to refuse. Equally, campesina girls, working as maids, are regarded as 'fair game' by the males of the household. So whether married or not, child-bearing begins at an early age. In the last general census in 1971, one-third of 14-year-old girls had already experienced at least one pregnancy.[5]

Notes

1. Isabel Nieve, 'Household Arrangements and Multiple Jobs in San Salvador', *Signs*, vol. 5, no. 1, p. 135.

2. The 1978 FUNDUSAL survey of the urban poor showed that 39.5% of households were headed by women.

3. Vilma Iraheta *et al.*, 'Escuela o Prisión? La organización social de un centro de orientación en El Salvador', *ECA*, año XXXVII, no. 401 (San Salvador, March 1982), pp. 179–92.

4. Latin American and Caribbean Women's Collective, *Slaves of Slaves: The Challenge of Latin American Women* (Zed Press, London, England, October 1980), pp. 148–9 is the first known published source to mention genital mutilation. The authors would like to thank Fran Hosken of Women's International Network, Lexington, Mass., for her extremely helpful comments on this matter.

5. Ibid., p. 148.

5 Family Planning

At the health centres in the country, the first thing they ask you is if you're using family planning and if you aren't, they won't give you any medicines for your children.
Campesina woman from Aguilares, San Salvador, April 1983

Salvadorean women are far from controlling their own fertility. Women can expect to have between five and eight children as a general rule, and in rural areas it is not uncommon for women to have up to 15 pregnancies.[1] The orthodox Catholic Church disapproves of the use of contraceptives and regards the state family planning programme as an attack on moral decency and a licence for sexual promiscuity. Men often oppose family planning, so many women must either hide the fact they are using birth control or meet with considerable opposition.

On the other hand, women are the targets of a mammoth campaign to persuade them to take up family planning on the grounds that large families are anti-social. Family planning as promoted in El Salvador has been characterized by very aggressive marketing and it is more than apparent that both the medical profession and women are subjected to unethical pressures.

El Salvador has suffered from one of the highest rates of population growth in the under-developed world. In 1978, it was estimated at 3.4% and various population planning agencies have therefore targeted the country for their attention.[2] They argue that disproportionate population growth lies at the root of the social and economic problems confronting the country at the present time:

The rapid population growth will continue to be the most fundamental problem for El Salvador in the long-term . . . A slower increase in population would allow the country to reach greater incomes per capita and a drop in fertility would imply a spectacular reduction of demands on public spending to satisfy people's basic needs, exemplified in the costs of education.[3]

The Salvadorean Demographic Association, an affiliate of the International Planned Parenthood Federation, claims that a three-child family should represent an absolute maximum. Larger families represent an unacceptable burden on the state or, worse still, may become enemies of society: 'All intelligent Salvadoreans – men or women – ought to realize that in order to get on in life, it is better to have one well-trained child, than 5 or 10 who are a burden, or enemies of the society in which we live.'[4]

State family planning programmes were first introduced in 1968 and since the establishment of the National Population Commission in 1974, they have become a major government priority. They have made the greatest impact in the metropolitan area of San Salvador but have found little acceptance in rural areas. The National Fertility Survey of 1978 found that 34% of all women of child-bearing age practised some form of contraception (56% in the metropolitan area, 42% in urban areas and 26% in rural areas).[5]

Drives to convince women to take up family planning use the mass media to the full. In San Salvador, children have picked up a catchy radio tune about the Condor brand of condoms and can be heard singing in the streets: 'Condor is your friend, – always take him with you!' Gynaecologists face heavy pressure to promote family planning:

> All medical staff are pressurized to force family planning on women. They are given certain targets or quotas to fulfil, depending on the kind of institution they work in. For instance, in the Maternity Hospital of San Salvador, we were told to perform a monthly average of 15 sterilizations per day.
> Dr Mario M, Mexico City, May 1983

Family planning Salvadorean fashion has become so notorious as to be classified as a human rights issue. At the 1976 US Congress hearings on human rights in El Salvador, Dr René Leon Schotter testified to the effect that: 'They are imposing birth control without the consent of the people involved. This is not family planning. This is a policy of the government against the population.'[6]

The most common form of family planning is irreversible sterilization. The National Fertility Survey found that out of the total of women using contraception, 52.5% had been sterilized. El Salvador has one of the highest percentages of women sterilized in the world and the question is raised as to how this has come about. In part, as Kate Young suggests:

> Women bear children in rapid succession when young and when they can no longer face the prospect of another child, they choose sterilization because it exempts them from having to take conscious and continuing responsibility for their own fertility in a culture which constantly denies women this right.[7]

But again psychological pressure is a very important factor:

> All women, even the very young, are put under pressure. At San Vicente Hospital, when I went to give birth, I met a young woman who had been coerced and she only had three children. In the hospital, at every

opportunity, the nurses would pass by and say: 'Why don't you get sterilized?' and they'd come back and say it again. 'There's no problem, you're better in a week and afterwards, your child will be well looked after, go to school, be better fed.'
Campesina woman, 28 years old, with two children, Mexico City, June 1982

While there are no confirmed reports of women who have been sterilized against their will or without their knowledge, many women have mentioned friends who have been sterilized without their permission and it is a common belief that it takes place. On the other hand, male sterilizations are rare and there is little promotion of the operation.

The pill is the most popular method of contraception because it is easiest to obtain and sold without restrictions in chemists. Injectable contraceptives, prohibited in most Western countries because of their proven association with an increased risk of cancer, are not widely used but are available.

7 different types of the drug (Depo-Provera) are still being sold as very effective forms of contraception with no side effects. The country's health authorities keep silent about the irreversible damages Depo-Provera can cause our women.[8]

The majority of doctors are simply not aware of the dangers attached to Depo-Provera and other injectable contraceptives, nor that they have been prohibited in other countries.

Health has never been a priority in the programmes. Women are not advised of the risks and the necessary check-up services are rarely available. Indeed, in factories in San Salvador, as one woman trade unionist reported, the pill is available from vending machines and instructions for use merely state: 'the pill should be taken once a day in order not to have more children' and conclude with the comforting advice 'if you don't feel well, there are other methods'. Many women have simply reached the conclusion that family planning methods prove too harmful to their health: 'I've seen the results: a lot of illnesses – especially cancer. Women all say they feel ill, whether using the pill or the coil' (campesina woman, San Vicente, April 1983).

Women regard the family planning programmes as a very mixed blessing. One 60-year-old campesina woman felt that her life would have been very different if family planning had been available in her day:

I had 14 children. During my youth, women didn't have the same expectations as they do today, nor were there methods for not having children. With less children, a woman can feel at peace, she doesn't get old so quickly as she hasn't got so much work. This is a great step forward and women can now be better educated.
San Salvador, April 1983

Generally speaking, however, family planning has met with a hostile reception. Women complain, not just about the pill, but the ideological package they are being asked to swallow:

> I think all this campaign is not because they are thinking about the interests of poor people, that's a lie. If a family is not using planning, in a year they have one child and in ten years, how many? At least five. Well, they reckon, this couple will get desperate and demand salary increases. But if the couple is using planning and only have one child, then 100 colones is enough to survive on. But in the countryside, we think that with lots of children, when you get old, they'll look after you.
> Campesina woman, San Salvador, April 1983

Suspicion of family planning in part reflects the influence of the Popular Church which has openly rejected the theory that the demographic explosion is the cause of El Salvador's economic and social problems. While the Popular Church has put particular emphasis on the natural method of birth control, it also runs various sex education programmes to explain the other methods. Its stated aim is to develop a greater degree of responsibility for pregnancies among both men and women and to allow them to make an informed choice.

On the left, the state programmes are criticized as imperialist population control, preventive genocide or 'another counter-insurgency mechanism'. On the whole, however, the left has given little priority to these issues. There are still few Salvadoreans who advocate the view that a woman's reproductive rights (or a right to self-determination based on a knowledge of her own sexuality) are fundamental to the development of a greater sense of autonomy and, in the long run, a wider political participation. Meanwhile, the state family planning programmes continue to treat women as objects whose fertility needs to be controlled rather than as people who might wish to exercise more control over their lives.

Notes

1. The 1971 census showed that the average number of live births per woman in urban areas was 5.7 and in rural areas 7.7. However, because of the high rate of infant mortality, the average number of live children per woman was 4.4 in urban areas and 5.6 in rural areas.

2. The population growth rate stood at 2.8% in the decade 1951–60, rose to 3.5% between 1961–71 and in 1978 was estimated at 3.4%. Luis Angel Rodríguez, *Quince años de labor en población y planificación* familiar (Asociación Demográfica Salvadoreña, El Salvador, 1977), p. 8.

3. *El Salvador: Demographic Questions and Perspectives*, World Bank Studies, Latin American and Caribbean Regional Office (World Bank, Washington, D.C., USA, October 1979), p. ii.

4. Rodríguez, *Quince años de labor*, p. 36.

5. 'Encuesta nacional de fecundidad, planificación familiar y comunicación masiva, El Salvador 1978', *FESAL 78* (Asociación Demográfica Salvadoreña, El Salvador, June 1980).

6. 'Human Rights in Nicaragua, Guatemala and El Salvador: Implications for US Policy, Hearings June 8–9', US House of Representatives Subcommittee on International Organizations of the Committee on International Relations, 1976, p. 74.

7. Minority Rights Group, *Latin American Women*, Report no. 57 (March 1983), p. 15.

8. *Salud en El Salvador – otra razón para el combate popular*, note 24, p. 61.

6 Women and Development

Now with our Women's Office, foreigners can see we're no longer a backward country.
Señora del Valle, Social Welfare Board, San Salvador Municipal Government, San Salvador, April 1983

The Political Constitution grants equal rights to women and men and, under President Duarte in 1981, the government ratified the United Nations Convention on the elimination of all forms of discrimination against women. However, when government and international planning agencies have turned their attention to the specific problem of 'development for women', it has been almost exclusively in terms of population control. Some policy statements, such as the 1974 'Integrated Population Policy', have argued for women's integration into the workforce and for increased educational opportunities, on the grounds that women's status is positively correlated with a reduction in fertility. On the other hand, some agencies recommend entirely the opposite:

> One of the policies proposed to reduce the large number of people looking for work and thus to reduce the level of unemployment, consists of ensuring that fewer women from the secondary population enter the labour market.[1]

The ILO here defines the secondary population as non-heads of households and considers women as dependants, arguing that resources should therefore be concentrated on the male population.

There has been little attempt to create projects to promote women's development and even less understanding of the issues involved. A survey of Central American women's development programmes carried out by the Mexican government's 'Women's Documentation Centre' in April 1982 produced from the Ministry of Education the following list of publications on women's issues available in El Salvador: *Vision Magazine*; *Today At Home*; *TV Guide*; *Vanity*; *Cosmopolitan*; *Good Housekeeping: The Status of Central American Women (1503–1821)* by Manuel Rubio Sánchez, Ministerio de Educación (n.d.). Heading the list of organizations concerned with women's development were the Girl Guides, the Izamar Centre (women's section of the Opus Dei) and the Association of Salvadorean Executive Secretaries.

During the United Nations International Women's Year in 1975, the Salvadorean government spent more time and much more money on ensuring that the Miss Universe beauty contest went off without a hitch, than on debating the issues of discrimination against women. While the Minister of Education was put in charge of selecting suitably personalized farewell gifts for each country's contestant, he did not see fit to put in an appearance at the National Co-ordinating Commission for International Women's Year. A series of conferences was arranged to pay homage to women's spirit of self-sacrifice, a pamphlet was published on women's legal rights and the year drew to a close.

Government ministries have done little to ensure that women's legal rights have been enforced. A notorious example is the Ministry of Labour, which is taking no action whatsoever to fight discrimination in the workplace although such work is in theory part of its brief. The Women's and Minors' Section at the Ministry of Labour employs a staff of five. They were very frank about the nature of their work with women:

> Our work with women is a bit limited, or rather, we hardly work with women at all. We neither investigate the problems women face at work, nor do we try and help. We have been thinking of changing the name of the office from 'Women and Minors' to 'Minors' only. We have asked to do so, but changes take a long time to come into effect. It seems that 15 or 20 years ago, women did come into the office with problems about maternity leave but they no longer come here. There is little we can do. We have a very limited budget and funds are being reduced all the time. Nor do we have the legal right to supervise work conditions in rural areas. Our control should be extended to the country and a tripartite commission exists to reform the Labour Code, but it was set up three years ago, and so far there haven't been any results.
>
> Sexual discrimination is, of course, very common, but it is difficult to detect and women don't make official complaints. There are laws against discrimination but to get them respected is another matter. We know of many violations of the Labour Code, women employed in hard physical labour which should legally be carried out by men. Just near here for example, in the distillery in the basement of the National Police Administration, there are a lot of women doing heavy manual labour. But if we were to intervene, the women would lose their jobs and they wouldn't thank us for that.
>
> Social worker, Women and Minors' Section, Ministry of Labour, San Salvador, April 1983

The Training Department of the Ministry of Labour has only organized three courses for women in the last decade and, as one study concludes, 'there is little interest in job training schemes for women'.[2]

Only recently has El Salvador caught up with the 'women and development' bandwagon and, in an attempt to modernize its image in the eyes of the rest of the world, on 7 March 1983, opened its 'Women's Office'. Both the initial idea and the financial backing came from the Inter-American Commission for Women (OAS dependency) and the project has been given no financial assistance from the government itself. The 'Women's Office' has been guaranteed a budget of US$20,000 over a period of two years, after which it will have to find financial backing from within the government. It is a Christian Democrat project, hopelessly under-financed and vague in its intentions. The office has no plans to tackle some of the most conspicuous discriminatory practices against women. For instance, it has no brief to propose a change in the law to give women wage parity in agricultural work because, as the Director of the Women's Office explained, that was the responsibility of the Women's and Minors' Section of the Ministry of Labour. The office has no grassroots support – indeed few women know of its existence. The project merely highlights the vacuous nature of women's development programmes as conceived in El Salvador at the present time.

Interview with Clara Luz Mendoza de Osorio, Director of the Women's Office

The Women's Office could hardly be described as pretentious – a partition carves off a very reduced space in a conference room on the top floor of the PGP and a hand-written sign announces its existence. Inside there is the secretary's desk, the Director's desk and three chairs for visitors – a filing cabinet is expected shortly. From here the Salvadorean government plans:

- to promote the participation of Salvadorean women in the educational, legal, social and economic fields in the short and long term;
- to co-ordinate public and private activities which promote women's integration in the social and economic development of the country;
- to establish permanent relations with national and international institutions or organizations which benefit women;
- to plan, design, and carry out programmes, collect information and documentation on women;
- to raise social awareness about the real capacities of women in order to facilitate their incorporation into the country's development;
- to maintain appropriate channels of communication in the media in order to inform people about women's projects;
- to ensure that the government carries out its national and international commitments to benefit women;
- to set up and maintain a permanent register on the legislation concerning women;
- to plan, draw up and carry out courses, seminars, conferences and other types of events aimed at women's development.

> Clara Luz Mendoza de Osorio looked up from reading this impressive list: 'My concern is to ensure that the proposed projects are carried out effectively. But the trouble is I have to do everything by myself' (San Salvador, April 1983).

Notes

1. PREALC, 'Situación y Perspectivas del Empleo en El Salvador' (International Labour Office, Chile, 1977), p. 19.

2. G: Lorena L. *et al., La Participación de la mujer en la economía salvadoreña, ante-proyecto de trabajo de investigación* (Facultad de Ciencias Económicas, Universidad Centroamericana 'José Simeon Cañas', San Salvador, March 1983).

Part 2: Sisters in Blood

7 The Popular Church

When a dictatorship seriously violates human rights and attacks the common good of the nation, when it becomes unbearable or closes all channels of dialogue, of understanding, of rationality, when this happens, the Church speaks of the legitimate right of insurrectional violence.
Archbishop Arnulfo Oscar Romero, San Salvador, 6 August 1979, *4th Pastoral Letter*

It is hard to under-estimate the influence of the Popular Church in the lives of Salvadorean women who have become involved in the opposition movement. For many it has been the crucial eye-opener, the starting-point for what many describe as the transformation of their lives and their commitment to revolutionary change. Particularly among the poor, in the shanty towns and in campesino communities, women have become actively critical of the government because of the influence of their church leaders. Many have been encouraged to join self-help organizations or trade unions through their church and from there have developed wider political commitments.

In El Salvador, the church has increasingly suffered from internal divisions between the Orthodox Church and the majority who have opted for the theology of liberation to form the 'Popular Church', whose most important exponent, until his murder, was Archbishop Romero.

The theology of liberation first developed in the 1960s as a Christian Socialist philosophy which holds that it is the duty of the Catholic Church to work for social and economic reforms, particularly in the Third World, and to adopt the cause of the oppressed. These positions were approved at a meeting of Latin American bishops in Medellín, Columbia, in 1968 and represented a watershed for the church in Latin America. The Medellín documents openly denounced the poverty and brutality of the relations of production in Latin America: withdrawing support from the classes in power the bishops called, most significantly, for agrarian reforms. The documents proposed programmes, based on the method of Paulo Freire's 'education for liberation', which were designed to promote a new sense of community action for change among the poor.

Adopting the theology of liberation, the main body of the Salvadorean church therefore became identified with opposition to the regimes in power during the 1970s. They produced a steady stream of protests on human rights violations and, criticizing the most apparent failings of the capitalist system and class society, sought to dispel the traditional fatalism of the poor. Their educational work in the local parishes and the Catholic campesino organization, FECCAS, proved to be extraordinarily successful.

The Christian Communities

The Christian communities (*Comunidades Cristianas de Base*) were initially small study groups set up by local parishes to discuss social problems and to try to find practical ways of solving them through community action. The groups also discussed personal values and relations and their wider political implications. They have predominantly attracted women and adolescents.

The church also set up a number of permanent rural communities where members of the Christian communities could go for weekend retreats or live there full-time.

Maria is one of the many examples of the younger generation who has become politically involved against the regime through her participation in a Christian community. She had been sent to an Orthodox Opus Dei school where religious education formed an important part of the curriculum. But, as she explained, she found that religion at her school was only designed to instil in her a sense of fear about sinning. When a friend invited her to attend one of the Christian community study groups, she was deeply impressed by the contrast and decided to join the community:

> We were a group of young people who all lived locally in one of the poorest areas on the outskirts of San Salvador. We began by studying the Bible and trying to relate what it said to our daily lives and the problems of the community. Perhaps they were simple questions but, at the age of 13, we felt we were beginning to think things out for ourselves. Why is it that there are rich and poor, that some people don't have homes or enough to eat? And instead of seeing it as something God had ordained, we began to look at the exploitation of the poor by the rich in a political way, but using Christian concepts.
>
> We began to organize to help the disadvantaged in the community. For instance, we raised enough money for the materials to build a decent house for a single mother who was living in a hut made of cardboard and we all worked together on the construction. And we tried to do something about the problem of alcoholism and prostitution in the area by getting the bars and brothels registered with the local government. But the more you try and get things done, the more you realize that the government doesn't care at all, apart from making a profit. And the more critical we became, the more we realized that the government might attack us. Together with some other

Christian communities, we had bought some land outside the city and some 300 families went to live and farm there. It was called 'El Paraíso' and was organized as a co-operative with all the work and profits shared. It was my idea of a truly authentic community. But then in 1980, it was attacked and many members were killed.

The government claimed we were subversives or terrorists. But our work had always been non-violent and non-partisan, that was one of our principles. Some of the members of our community had taken the decision to join the mass political organizations or the armed struggle but that was their personal choice and the community never expressed an opinion on the subject. I decided to work with the market women's organization, ASUTRAMES, because my mother had a market stall and I would help her, and because the community had taught me how important it was to claim our rights.
Maria, refugee in Mexico City, October 1982

The Christian communities were most active during the period in which Mñs Romero was Archbishop of San Salvador (1977–80):

> Mñs Romero called upon us to join a community and share the lives of the poor. We were given detailed programmes of work, which included visiting families and working alongside them so as to be able to understand their most pressing difficulties. We would hold discussions about national politics, to look at the lack of civil liberties and to examine how the system of exploitation divides one person from another. We didn't provide any answers but let the community reach its own conclusions.
>
> We used the Medellín documents as our guide and behind the discussions was our belief that only with structural changes in society could we form a truly Christian society, which to our way of thinking would also be a socialist society.
> Sister Lucero, Mexico City, December 1982

The Changing Place of Women in the Popular Church

The Salvadorean Popular Church has placed particular emphasis on the need to promote women's equality, both in terms of the traditional exclusion of women religious workers from certain liturgical responsibilities and in society in general: 'Women of course have played a subordinate role within the Church but Mñs Romero took up our cause. He allowed nuns to carry out baptisms, give communions, all of which was unheard of before' (Sister Lucero).

While more women than men have always been active members of the church, at the present time, this situation has been accentuated:

> On the whole, men are more involved in the political organizations and women at the grassroots level, particularly in the Christian communities. The political organizations require a full time and very disciplined commitment which it is difficult for women with children to fulfil. They therefore prefer to take part in church work.
> Sister Asunción, Mexico City, February 1983

In the Christian communities, the church has encouraged women to take an active role in community politics and has promoted more egalitarian relations within the family. The rural development centre CEPROR (*Centro de Promoción Rural*) ran special courses for young women. Sister Asunción, who was in charge of the programme over a period of two years (1975–7), helped train approximately 2,000 young women in community work. CEPROR offered general courses on health, nutrition, community organization and, for women, included a special course entitled: 'What does it mean to be a woman?'

> The main aim of the course was to help women overcome their feelings of inadequacy and to make them realize that they were equally capable of becoming community leaders. So we would examine socially determined personality differences between the sexes, why it is that men are always seen to be the intellectuals, things like that. They were important discussions as women often feel that community action is a mystery to them and that the only thing they can really understand is looking after the kids. I think the courses were a success because many campesina women became important leaders afterwards.
> Sister Asunción

In the Christian communities, discussions on personal relations between both men and women placed emphasis on the need to make men more responsible for their families and take an equal part in domestic work.

> As Christians we believe in freedom and equality between the sexes. Men as a rule are very selfish and still believe that women are born to serve them. They are terribly irresponsible and spend all their free time drinking with their friends. And women are as likely as not to be left to fend for themselves, living crowded into one room with all the children and having to work all night sewing or cleaning to make ends meet. We're trying our best to strengthen the family and make men more conscious of women's rights. And let me tell you, if there was a women's demonstration to protest against the machismo of the men in our country, I'd be right there in the front ranks!
> Sister Ana, San Salvador, April 1983

The Church in Opposition

From 1977 onwards, when Archbishop Romero took office, the church became increasingly identified with the opposition to General Romero's regime (no relation) and subsequently the military juntas and the Christian Democrat Party. Although formerly the Christian Democrats had found an important support base within the church, this was gradually withdrawn. Lay members of the church moved with their religious leaders to condemn the 'institutionalized violence' of the oligarchy and now offer both political and practical support to the opposition.

The church's success in mobilizing support through FECCAS for far-reaching agrarian reforms in 1976, coupled with the outspoken criticism of the regime coming from the Catholic university, UCA, provoked the wrath of the government-backed paramilitary groups. Accusing the church of Communist subversion, they inaugurated a persecution campaign. The White Warrior's Union (UGB), one of the most notorious paramilitary groups, declared that all Jesuit priests in the country were on their death list and anonymous leaflets were put into circulation which suggested: 'Be a Patriot – Kill a Priest'. Foreign priests were expelled from the country and between February and May 1977 alone, 17 priests were expelled from the country or forced into exile, 4 were imprisoned and tortured and 6 killed. Lay members of the church were also murdered and, in May 1977, the Christian community centre at Aguilares was bombed by the army and an estimated 300–400 civilians murdered.

While the persecution of the Popular Church was basically instigated by the government, a small group of religious dignitaries, with tacit backing from the Papal Nuncio, joined the attack on liberation theologians, condemning them as tantamount to heretics. Right-wing clergy have either kept silent on the issue of human rights or bracketed those who speak out as supporters of subversion.

The papacy has been content to issue periodic exhortations in favour of peace and understanding which, in the context of the wholesale slaughter of priests and laymen, amounts to an abdication of all responsibility. The Pope's visit to Central America in March 1983 did nothing to alter this situation.

In response to these attacks, Archbishop Romero refused to attend the inauguration of the new president, General Romero, claiming he had a more important engagement with the people, an adroit reference to the huge fraud and violence which had accompanied the elections. In his sermons, broadcast over the radio, the Archbishop condemned the paramilitary groups as part of the institutionalized violence which could not be rooted out without reforms to create more just economic and social structures. The church became increasingly involved with human rights work: Romero made a practice of announcing the week's toll of human rights violations at his packed Sunday sermons and the *Socorro Jurídico*, the Archbishop's legal aid office, became an internationally recognized source of independent information on the repression.

After the October 1979 coup, Archbishop Romero declared that the new regime lacked any popular backing and could only count on the support of a 'few foreign powers'. Condemning US military aid to the regime, he wrote an open letter to President Carter asking him to withdraw his support. Significantly for the church, he criticized the PDC presence in the military juntas and stated that they were only being used to cover up its repressive military character.

Before he was murdered on 24 March 1980, Romero made two fundamental statements: he declared that the church supported the legitimate right to insurrectional violence against a dictatorship in August 1979 and, only a day before he was shot dead while holding a mass in San Salvador, he called on members of the army and security forces to refrain from shooting if it ran contrary to their conscience.

Romero's murder, into which there has still been no official investigation, was most probably instigated by Roberto D'Aubuisson, leader of the ARENA Party. Romero became El Salvador's uncanonized martyr and his funeral was attended by 80,000 mourners, some one-fifth of the country's resident population. The televised ceremony was attacked by army troops and over 40 people killed, to the irrevocable discredit of the regime. The political affinity between the Popular Church and the organized opposition to the regime was firmly sealed when the CRM, forerunner to the FDR, called a two-week protest general strike.

The persecution of the church has continued since Romero's murder. The rape and murder of four US churchwomen who were carrying out humanitarian work with the displaced in December 1980 has received the most detailed international press coverage, but it is by no means an isolated case. Salvadorean nuns and lay workers have also been raped and murdered and many more have been forced into exile. Sister Lucero has been arrested on a number of occasions and is now in exile. Sister Asunción's convent was completely destroyed by a bomb attack, although luckily the community had been warned and everyone had gone into hiding. She too is now in exile.

Because the risks involved are now too great, much of the work of the Christian communities has been abandoned, but religious and lay followers of the Popular Church consider that Romero remains their spiritual leader and continue to provide important support to the opposition:

> Now we have to work secretly but if it weren't for the repression the Communities would be much bigger. At our Sunday Mass, you can see how we all come together to express our silent opposition to the regime. We all know why we are there. But there is a constant control and you go to bed not knowing if they might not come for you in the night. Only recently one of our compañeras, her husband and his two brothers were all killed in their beds. We have to keep moving from house to house, because nowhere is safe. There are always police spies around the Church.
>
> Irene, Christian Community, San Salvador, April 1983

The communities continue to carry out humanitarian work with the displaced and in the hospitals. Many are directly helping the controlled zones with food and clothing.

Now in exile, Sister Guadalupe recently returned to El Salvador on a brief visit, although she knows she is on many paramilitary death lists.

She visited her rural community after two years' absence and was impressed by the degree of collective organization and determination shown by her community.

> The control exercised by ORDEN is terrifying and everyone has to be extremely careful. But none the less the community is expressing support for the FDR–FMLN in ways which it is really surprising to see. They manage to get food sent through to the controlled zones and I saw a van come back laden with fruit which the compañeros had sent them in return. And they have held their own popular vote, not in an assembly, as that would have been too dangerous, but going round the community asking their opinion, so now they have 'elected' a very courageous woman whom they want to be their Mayoress when the FDR–FMLN take power.
> Mexico City, May 1983

The new Archbishop Rivera y Damas remains outspoken on human rights violations and continues much of the legal work sponsored by the former Archbishop. However, he is regarded as a less vocal critic of the government, has banned the study of the Medellín documents and asked nuns and priests to withdraw from their community work on the grounds that it had become too dangerous:

> It was a problem for us as many were reluctant to return to our convents or seminaries. It felt like abandoning all the people we had been working with, whom we had been encouraging to organize and demand their rights. Some nuns and priests chose to go into the FMLN controlled zones where they are not only carrying out religious work but also helping in the educational campaigns. Others are working with the displaced in the internal refuges run by the church. But the emphasis of our work has changed and the training that nuns are receiving now is very different from the formation I received, less concerned with education for liberation.
>
> I have been forced into exile but maintain my work with the refugee community in Mexico City. I openly support the FDR–FMLN and feel that it would be an opportunistic attitude on my part to expect to act as a spiritual leader of my people after the triumph of the revolution if I were not working with them at this crucial time.
> Sister Guadalupe

8 Women and the Trade Unions

The first time we went on strike in 1976 to obtain a collective contract, the North American manager said to the strike committee: 'You don't need a trade union here – this is a factory full of women!'
Sonia López, Secretary of Women's Affairs, FENASTRAS, Mexico City, May 1982

The Salvadorean trade union movement has always suffered from brutal repression; there has never been freedom to organize. Today, more than ever, unionists are under threat. Activists are illegally dismissed, strikes are forcibly broken up by the army or police and many unionists have been killed. The great majority of unions therefore have to operate secretly.

The Labour Code was introduced in 1950 and, for the first time, urban unions were officially permitted – although they had to be legally recognized by the Ministry of Labour. Agricultural workers were still denied the right to organize, a situation which continues today.

Trade Union Law

Article 205 of the Labour Code prohibits: 'Discrimination against workers on the grounds of their trade union activities or reprisals against them for the same motive.'

Article 528 Par. 3 of the Labour Code states: 'In matters concerning labour, recognized strikes are those which have as their aim the defence of the common professional interests of the workers.'

The Labour Code declares solidarity strikes illegal.

The Labour Code has never been interpreted in the interests of the working class. Sanctions against employers who discriminate on the grounds of trade union activities are minimal fines which are rarely enforced in practice. The Ministry of Labour always recognizes a just cause for dismissal as long as the correct indemnity pay is given and only three strikes have been officially declared legal since the passing of the Code in 1950.

The present state of siege has suspended all constitutional guarantees, including the right to strike.

Rural Trade Unions

Rural trade unions do not feature in official statistics as they are considered illegal. However, the organization of rural workers has been crucial to the formation of the Salvadorean opposition movement and political repression has been most savage in the countryside. FECCAS, the Catholic rural federation, was founded in 1971. In 1974 it formed an alliance with the left-wing rural workers' union, the UTC. Both were founding members of the popular organization, the BPR, in 1975. At this time, both FECCAS and the UTC had a membership of around 6,000.

The North American federation, AIFLD, promoted the organization of peasant co-operatives through the UCS. The goals of this movement were to seek minimal economic improvements while preventing campesinos from looking for more radical solutions. In contrast, the demands of the FECCAS–UTC included the key question of agrarian reform, the right to land, together with other issues such as the reduction of land rents, higher minimum wages and better credit facilities. In early 1977, for the first time in 30 years, campesinos in the central region of the country occupied land from which they had been evicted over a long period of time to make way for export crops. In October of the same year, the major rural trade unions presented a joint demand for increased wages in harvest work. This campaign reached a peak in November when the Ministry of Labour was occupied.

In 1978, there were further land occupations organized by the FECCAS–UTC, now renamed the FTC, particularly in the north and central regions. Some occupations were to last for almost six months, but the end results were always the same: army operations to destroy the crops and the murder of the leaders involved.

> The work of FECCAS was wonderful to see. We began in 1977. A member of the Federation, one of the richer people around there, who had taken our side, rented some lands to FECCAS so we could work them in co-operatives. We grew maize, rice, beans and sesame. We shared the beans out among the sick and the poor from our canton, who didn't even have a plot of land of their own. And we would organize collective work, so that, for example, if someone had a plot which needed clearing, we would all go and lend a hand. I would help with the preparation of a meal for all the men who were doing the work. It was really lovely to see how everyone helped everyone else.
> Susana Prieto, México City, June 1983

In Susana's canton, Portillo de Norte, near the River Lempa in Chalatenango, about 80% of the population of 3,000 were affiliated to FECCAS. She was involved in a land occupation near the river:

> In the first place, we asked for a salary rise, a reduction in land rents and more fertile land because usually the owners round there would rent us plots

which weren't good for anything. We went on strike in support of our demands but nothing came of it. So we decided to occupy some unused land owned by Don Juan López, the big landowner of our region. We worked very hard in the fields for about four months. We cultivated maize and water melons and the crops were just about ripe when the army came one night without warning and destroyed everything. They captured all the FECCAS leaders. They didn't find my husband at home but I was there and they beat me terribly. They even put a rifle in my mouth and threatened to kill me. They tied me up, ransacked the house and burnt our grain store. They killed an enormous number of people that night because nearly the whole canton had joined FECCAS. The repression there became well known. Four days later, Mñs Romero came to visit us. He held a special mass and gave me and another woman some money so we could go to see a doctor because we had both been so badly beaten.

We had to move into the capital afterwards, because we feared they would come back to look for my husband and I began to suffer from my nerves, thinking about all I had seen. They killed my husband in the end, in 1982. He was found near Aguilares, naked, nothing but his body. We never found his head. Soon afterwards I had to leave the country.

Another rural trade union, the UNJ, formed in 1979, organized rural day labourers in the departments of San Salvador and Chalatenango. They formulated a series of demands which included equal pay for women. A campesina woman who had been forced to move into the capital because her brother had been taken a political prisoner, had participated in the UNJ:

We fought to make the work quotas lighter and for salary rises, for a free mid-day meal, for women and children to get a full salary. All of which seemed just to me. We presented these demands to the estate administrator but he ignored them. So we decided to stop working until our demands were met. The administrator phoned the estate owner and brought in the National Guard who captured the leaders of the union from their homes one night. Everyone who was in the union was either killed or captured. My brother has now spent more than two years in prison.

Marta, Committee of Mothers, San Salvador, April 1983

Agrarian Reform

Agrarian reform when it was finally announced in March 1980 was not just a question of too little too late. A Washington initiative hurriedly pushed through to undermine support for the campesino organizations, the project was conceived as part of a wider counter-insurgency programme. In itself, the reform suffered from a number of insuperable flaws: designed from above, it had a tiny support base in the heavily decimated Christian Democrat Party and was drawn up without consultation or reference to El Salvador's land tenure patterns. Most important, its implementation relied on the military, who, in the overwhelming majority, were adamantly anti-reform.

Agrarian Reform Law

The Agrarian Reform Law (Decree 153, March 1980) called for the expropriation of large estates, the first phase to cover lands over 500 hectares and the second, those between 100–150 hectares. Owners were to be compensated through bonds and the expropriated lands were to be converted into communal holdings run by the resident labour force or *colonos*. Estates over 500 hectares accounted for only some 15% of all agricultural lands while Phase II would have much wider implications, affecting as much as 70% of all coffee estates.

Phase III (Decree 207, April 1980) known as the 'Land to the Tiller' programme, gave renters the right to buy the land they worked – over a 30-year repayment period but with immediate property ownership. Based on plans worked out for the Asian landscape, where large absentee owners rented small plots to campesino families, it failed to make the simple observation that in El Salvador, most rented land consists of small plots of the most marginal soil and is owned by campesino families. This phase would merely put an end to a fairly flexible system of land use, often between members of the same extended family. The right of ownership over tiny plots of land, the majority too small to support a family's subsistence needs and where continued use would result in soil exhaustion, could not improve El Salvador's grave land distribution problems. Nor did the envisaged reform programme address the plight of no less than 50% of the rural population, who are neither resident labourers nor have access to rented lands.

Phase II and Phase III were never really implemented: the former was indefinitely suspended because it seriously attacked the landed oligarchy's interests; the latter, because it was simply not feasible, given the labyrinthine pattern of these minute holdings and the lack of any adequate national land survey. Phase I, on the other hand, was partially implemented and reportedly 265 estates over 500 hectares were turned into co-operatives. But this process went hand in glove with a virtual military invasion of the countryside and was conducted under a state of siege declared the day after the announcement of the reform programme, not to be lifted until the March 1982 elections. Above all, the reform was used by the right-wing military and paramilitary to identify and then kill campesino activists, in an effort to destroy all organized opposition in the countryside.

Jorge Alberto Villacorta, Under-Secretary for Agriculture, provided evidence of these murders when he resigned on 26 March 1980, some three weeks into the reform programme:

> During the first days of the reform – to cite one case – five directors and two presidents of the new campesino organizations were assassinated and I am informed that this repressive practice continues to increase. Recently, on one of the *haciendas* of the agrarian reform, uniformed members of the security forces accompanied by someone with a mask over his face, brought the workers together; the masked man was giving orders to the person in charge of the troops and these campesinos were gunned down in front of their co-workers.[1]

In the first year of the programme, more than 500 campesino leaders were murdered. The reform operated as a green light for a rural pacification campaign which was increasingly to encompass civilians not associated with any campesino organization or the armed struggle. This government 'scorched earth policy' is reminiscent of the worst atrocities of the Vietnam War. Designed to destroy local support for the FMLN forces, whole communities have been erased from the map. Not only have vital subsistence crops been burnt but civilians have been brutally murdered as part of a deliberate policy to create terror and clear the regions where the FMLN operate.

By the end of 1982, the FTC membership had dropped significantly to around 40,000. Many members had been killed or forced to flee into the cities and many more had joined the FMLN. The FTC now estimates that some 80% of all FMLN combatants are campesinos and former members of their organization.

Women's Rights and the Rural Trade Unions

It is largely because of the work of the Popular Church that campesina women have not been excluded from rural trade unions but encouraged to participate. Although they usually work as collaborators, helping with the meals for example, some women have become important leaders:

> Ticha was one of the most active leaders in Aguilares. FECCAS had formed a branch there and she helped organize women coffee harvesters. She took part in a number of land occupations and later went to the capital to work for FECCAS there. But she became too well known and received too much support and the paramilitary murdered her eventually.
> Sister Guadalupe, Mexico City, June 1982

Generally speaking, it is less common for a woman to join a rural than an urban trade union and women who do participate are not so conscious of their exploitation at work and in the home. Not all radical campesino and rural workers' unions have specifically addressed the question of women's rights or even equal pay, but there is a growing recognition of the need to do so. For instance, the FTC has recognized the importance of women's participation and has condemned women's oppression:

> The Federation of Rural Workers, FTC, manifests its abhorrence of the oppression to which women are subjected in all of Latin America. The anti-popular regimes commit innumerable injustices against women: from marginalization in the workplace and physical violence to the transnationals' policy of using women in mass media propaganda.
>
> Central American women have become conscious of their situation and understand that the revolution for permanent liberation is the fundamental solution to the grave problems that they confront.[2]

The Urban Trade Unions

In the 1970s, growing rank and file militancy, spurred by the steady decline in real wages, led to a move to surpass the cautious policies of the government-backed *Confederación General de Sindicatos* (CGS). Important industrial sectors, including public workers in power and water services, broke from the CGS to form independent federations, either directly or indirectly influenced by the new popular organizations. While in 1971 the CGS controlled 42% of all unionized workers, by 1976 its share had dropped to 19%.[3] The Romero regime (1977–9) responded to this growing militancy with the introduction of a Public Order Law which effectively banned strike action. Despite this, the independent unions continued to call for strikes and became increasingly involved in political protest.

After the October 1979 coup, disillusionment with the possibility of achieving reform through participation in the new government rapidly set in. In the first month of the new junta, 131 workers were reported killed as the military hardliners in government sought to clamp down on the unions. General strikes were called in March, June and August of 1980, accompanied by civil protests in the cities. For the period October 1979–December 1981 alone, the CDHES lists over 8,000 cases of trade unionists who were arrested, killed or had disappeared.

In July and August of 1980, the Duarte regime introduced a series of decree laws restricting all trade union activities: public employees were forbidden to strike and major public sectors were simply conscripted by decree into the armed forces and placed under military discipline. Decree 507, the new Public Order Law, prohibited all collective bargaining and strike action.

Since the March 1982 elections, the decree laws have all remained in force, despite a united trade union protest calling for their withdrawal. The trade union movement has reached a new unity with the foundation of the *Comité Unitario Sindical* (CUS) which calls for a negotiated solution in common with the FDR–FMLN position. Trade union activity is gradually gathering strength again after a period in which it had been almost impossible to act publicly. Despite the prohibitions, even public employees are taking strike action, including members of the Ministry of Agriculture, Public Works and the Social Security Institute and have received wide support from other sectors. On May Day 1983, a number of trade union federations held congresses openly in San Salvador for the first time since 1980.

The Fight for Trade Union Recognition

Women are severely under-represented in the urban trade union movement and make up under one-quarter of the total membership. However, they have been very active in the large multinational textile and assembly factories which employ women almost exclusively. Most of these trade unions are of recent creation, founded in the mid or late 1970s and are affiliated to federations organized by the mass political organizations.

In the free industrial zones, trade unions were unofficially banned and the government refused to recognize the unions that were formed, although they fulfilled the legal requirements. Women were therefore forced either to go on strike or to occupy factories in order to gain the right to a collective contract and recognition of their union. Examples of the repressive treatment women strikers received abound.

At IMES, a North American multinational textile factory employing some 300 women, five women leaders were dismissed illegally when the workforce formed a union in 1978. When the factory was occupied in protest, the Ministry of Labour declared the strike illegal and the occupation was forcibly broken up a week later. By then, the women had all become firm trade union supporters, staged solidarity strikes with a number of other factories and political stoppages to protest at the arrest of important opposition leaders.

In May 1979, because of the militancy of its workforce, IMES decided to close down the plant and move elsewhere. It announced the suspension of all work on the grounds of lack of raw materials. Recognizing a manoeuvre on the part of the company to avoid indemnity pay, the workers occupied the factory. They remained in occupation until 16 October 1979, immediately after the coup against Romero, when the factory warehouse was burnt down by the company and the women dislodged by armed members of the Treasury Police. They received no indemnity pay and the factory was closed. The majority of these women have remained unemployed and are now working for the opposition movement in a variety of ways.

At Eagle International, an American glove factory, the trade union was unofficially formed in 1972. Prior to 1978, when the factory was relocated in the San Bartolo industrial park, there were three strikes for official trade union recognition. In the 1976 strike, 50 North American guards were sent to dislodge the women from the factory gates. The US manager, who knew no Spanish, had been taken hostage and had phoned the embassy claiming he had been captured by Communists. In 1977, there was another strike: the day after the workers occupied the factory, they were forcibly evicted by members of the armed forces, the National Guard and the Treasury Police, who used tear-gas bombs against them. In the negotiations after the eviction, the women won the right to a collective contract and the reinstatement of 90 workers who had been dismissed.

In 1978, when the factory moved, the union was officially dissolved although it continued to function secretly. There were 490 members of the union and the nine-member Executive Committee were all women. The women of Eagle were nicknamed the 'Clenched Fists of Gloves' on account of their militancy and solidarity with other trade unions. They claimed to be the first all-women trade union to strike for recognition and their cause is well known in El Salvador because – as they describe it – they had to fight the 'marines'!

Women Trade Union Leaders

Women leaders of the militant trade unions possess a strong sense of their exploitation both as workers and as women. Many have been forced to leave husbands who have refused to let them participate in trade union activities. One branch organizer from the sweets and pasta union, *Sindicato de Trabajadores de la Industria de Dulces y Pastas* (SIDPA), outlined some of the difficulties she had encountered in organizing her factory:

> Many women realized that our trade union didn't have the support of the management and believed it couldn't resolve any of our problems. Another negative influence was religion. In our country, there are many religious sects, such as the Evangelists and the Jehovah's Witnesses, who do not have a policy of commitment to the poor and oppose trade union organization. The other problem we faced, which was the most serious, was that the management had created their own trade union. SIDPA was an independent union. Management always kept a track on all the workers and treated those of us in the independent union very differently. For instance, they wouldn't give you loans except on condition you left the independent union. And also the boss or the supervisors would treat you badly if you were active in our union. They'd give you low-paying jobs, reduce your salary or simply dismiss you with no reasons given.
> Magdalena, SIDPA Representative, Mexico City, May 1982

The former Secretary of Women's Affairs of FENASTRAS, Sonia López, who died in tragic circumstances in the autumn of 1983 in exile in Mexico City, was a young woman with only secondary education. She felt work with women was indispensable, not only for the trade union movement but as part of a longer educational process which would enable women to participate fully after the triumph of the FDR–FMLN.

My work was primarily with women in the manufacturing industries and I worked in Eagle International before I became a full-time organizer. The industrial parks were the worst. Trade unions were not permitted and San Bartolo free zone was like entering a prison – there was barbed wire fencing around the site and a special security force in operation. They kept a check on all our activities.

As Secretary of Women's Affairs, my work was to fight for laws to protect and aid women workers. FENASTRAS was the first trade union federation to really take the question of women's rights seriously. We made demands for a cheap canteen on the site, for nurseries and better maternity provisions. We also campaigned against the widespread practice of pregnancy tests by employers and the dismissal of pregnant women. We took up cases of sexual harassment as well, although it was difficult. If the Federation took up a case, it often meant that the worker in question was dismissed on some pretext, accused of robbery for example. And each company had their own labour lawyer who knew how to fix things in their favour.

We organized courses for women trade union leaders. We discussed the problems women had in becoming active, difficulties with husbands and the problems of child-care. We also held meetings with women from other sectors, such as campesina and market women, so that we could exchange experiences and ideas.

But it was a very difficult period. As the repression increased, more and more of our time was spent denouncing human rights violations. And it wasn't just the management we were fighting but the army and the security forces as well. There's no such thing as impartial arbitration in El Salvador. The army, government and the companies are all against the worker. I had to leave the country because of death threats and Mercedes Recinos, who worked in the post before me, was murdered. She was only 21 years old when killed and had been extraordinarily dedicated to our cause. She began to work at our factory at the age of 16. She helped to get the 90 workers reinstated that year. Then she was fired and taken to court, charged with intent to damage property and the possession of arms. The entire thing was entirely trumped up and she was absolved because of the publicity we gave the case. But rather than have Mercedes back in the factory, the company preferred to pay her wages through the Ministry of Labour and wouldn't let her return to work or even come near the factory. She became Secretary of Women's Affairs in 1978 and was killed in May 1979 by the security forces. She'd gone to visit her parents in Chalatenango and nine armed men in a jeep just drove up and shot her right in front of her parents.

Elsy Márquez, my successor in the job, has also been captured and disappeared since August 1981. She was picked up in the centre of town in broad daylight. FENASTRAS has carried out a huge campaign to try and get her released and produce almost weekly protests against her disappearance in the main newspapers of San Salvador. She has two children and was 24 years old when captured.

Sonia López, FENASTRAS, Mexico City, June 1982

FENASTRAS Demands the Liberty of Elsy Márquez

The National Trade Union Federation of Salvadorean Workers, FENASTRAS, demands the liberty of Elsy Márquez, Secretary of Women's Affairs on our General Executive Committee. Our *compañera*, according to witnesses, is in the hands of the Security Forces and has been deprived of her liberty for 209 days.

To this date, the Governing Junta and Supreme Court of Justice, through Judge No. 12 of Military Hearings, have not proceeded to hand over her case to the civil courts.

UNITY, SOLIDARITY AND STRUGGLE
Executive Committee, FENASTRAS

Source: *El Mundo*, San Salvador, 10 March 1982

Notes

1. Quoted in James Dunkerley, *The Long War* (London, Junction Books, 1982), p. 155.

2. 'La Mujer Centroamericana', *FTC Boletín Internacional*, no. 2 (1983), p. 5.

3. *The Long War*, p. 59.

9 Market Women

On the 23rd February 1921, government forces gunned down a demonstration of market women in San Salvador. But far from being cowed by this event, the market women picked up their dead and wounded, armed themselves with stones, sticks and knives and counter-attacked. They even took over the small police station in the El Calvario district, the nearest to the main market, and executed a number of the constables who had taken part in the massacre. The women who worked in the butchers' section distinguished themselves the most during that very special battle.
Roque Dalton, *Miguel Marmol* (EDUCA, Costa Rica, February 1982), p. 94

Market saleswomen have always been the most aggressive because they get the roughest end of the stick. We have it very clear in our minds that 'Union is Strength'.
Radio Venceremos Transcripts: 'Interviews with Women', January 1982

Women comprise the vast majority of the market workforce, which has represented an important political force of the opposition movement in this century. Today, the market women have formed a number of organizations, including the *Asociación de Usuarios y Trabajadores de los Mercados de El Salvador* (ASUTRAMES), which is affiliated to the FDR.

These women are at the heart of the economy – markets are the main centres for the wholesale and retail distribution of a huge variety of goods and the market workforce can exercise considerable political muscle, as their taxes are one of the main sources of income for the local government. Markets are also important social centres. Their small eating places, serving the cheapest meals and snacks in each town, are always crowded. Here people gather to gossip, exchange information and comment on current affairs. It is common in El Salvador for political campaigners to hold meetings outside markets, where they can always be assured of a large audience.

Market women are proverbially tough. They are women who have learnt to defend themselves, who are directly affected by central and local government policies, price speculation and the economic situation of the country. Many have a clear sense of class, recognizing themselves as the exploited, subjected to the petty extortion and corruption of the market administration, the police and other security forces. For these reasons, they have an enormous sense of solidarity with popular protest movements, trade unionists and political prisoners.

Marketing is the single largest category of female employment, straddling both the informal and formal sectors. San Salvador has five main retail markets with a total of 8,000 stalls and one wholesale market. The Central Market has eight buildings, all with two storeys and a basement, and some estimates claim that as many as 10,000 people work in and around the buildings. But there is no way of knowing the true numbers – women come and go, depending on their economic circumstances.

Profit margins are low, even for the better-off market sellers, who can afford to rent stalls. The consumer spending crisis has forced many women to close down their businesses. Street sellers are the worst off. Their profits are minimal. The poorest buy goods on a daily credit basis at high interest rates and, if they are unsuccessful with their sales, are forced to lower their prices towards the end of the day so as to have enough to pay back the loan.

Work hours can be very long and, as they are self-employed, the women have no labour rights such as holiday pay or health insurance. Many live in the squalid shanty towns around San Salvador, far from their work:

> We lived in the San Ramón district on the outskirts of the city. It took us about an hour by bus to get into the Central Market but in the last year we were there, the public transport system collapsed and we had to go home in trucks just as if we were cattle. The majority of the houses in the neighbourhood lacked both electricity and running water. I had to go and fetch water from two blocks away at 5 a.m. before setting off to the market. I would get back from work absolutely exhausted.
>
> Our house was small and only had two rooms. There was no kitchen but then we always ate at the market. There were 11 of us living there, my uncle and his family and my mother and sisters.
>
> Maria, Central Market canteen owner's daughter, Mexico City, October 1982

Most markets still do not possess a proper building. Instead, they are either covered with a corrugated iron roof or are in the street. Each market is administered by the local government, which fixes tariffs for renting stalls in the buildings and rates for services, such as gas and electricity. The market administration is responsible for the maintenance of the building or site, rubbish collection, security and rents. Tariffs are high and credit facilities for vendors are normally controlled by the administration. Misuse of funds is routine practice.

The New Municipal Markets of San Salvador

In the mid-1970s, the major markets of San Salvador were reconstructed.

Napoleón Duarte, elected Mayor of San Salvador in 1969, began the scheme and promised that the new buildings would transform working conditions and pull the market women out of their poverty. But when completed, the tariff rates had risen astronomically, in some cases by over 1000%.

The new markets became a source of intense political fighting between the PCN and the PDC, with accusations of embezzlement and corruption flying back and forth. Both parties tried to organize support for their position, but the great majority of market women supported the Society of Women Market Vendors, an independent organization formed to oppose the new tariff system. Some 2,000 market women, members of the society, filled the public galleries of the Legislative Assembly when the new tariffs were under discussion in June 1975. 'The Congressional Deputies had to shout over the loud-speaker so as to be heard above the noisy protest of hundreds of women market stallholders who filled the public galleries.'[1] The women believed that the PDC's stated concern for their welfare was nothing but a hollow promise:

> The new buildings didn't help the market workers because when they were opened we had to pay much higher rates for everything – we even had to pay to go to the bathroom. We got nothing out of it, while the Mayor and the government pocketed all the profits.
> Ana Eugenia, ASUTRAMES representative, Mexico City, September 1982

While the Society of Women Market Vendors exposed the corruption of the PDC and objected to the high tariffs in the new markets, it was not sufficiently organized to form a counter-proposal or take action upon it.

The Co-ordinating Committee of Market Women 'Luz Dilian Arévalo'

The Co-ordinating Committee of Market· Women 'Luz Dilian Arévalo', founded in 1978, organized market women for solidarity work, mainly on human rights issues and held political meetings in the markets to denounce the government. The committee has now become a part of the Association of Women of El Salvador (AMES). It was named after a young 20-year-old member of the Committee after she was killed by the army in a demonstration of 8 May 1979. Another active member, Laura, was also killed in 1981.

The Committee has worked closely with political prisoners. José Antonio Morales Carbonell, son of the ex-Mayor of San Salvador, who was captured by the security forces on 13 June 1980 and remained imprisoned for almost two years, recalls the solidarity of these market women in his testimony given to the CDHES:

[In Santa Tecla Penal Centre] the food continued to be

terrible and not only caused malnutrition but also gastro-
entiritic illnesses. We decided to write to the market women,
asking them if they could help with food supplies and telling
them why we were forced to ask for their assistance. The
following day, the response of these women was tremendous.
They brought all kinds of food which we were able to prepare
into a very nutritious meal for all of us, with milk, bread, meat,
eggs and fruit; and we notified the head of the prison that on that
day, we would not require the official 'food'. We organized
cooking, cleaning and distribution brigades and demonstrated
our efficiency, organization and responsibility. As a result, the
following day, they improved our food.[2]

Women from the Committee have been arrested, their homes
ransacked and their families persecuted because of their work for
political prisoners.

ASUTRAMES

Because the market women became known for their opposition to the
regime, the larger markets were heavily infiltrated by members of the
security forces. In the Central Market in San Salvador, the manager,
General Noel Aparicio, created a special uniformed and armed
vigilante force to intimidate the market women. 'It got to the point where
we felt we were entering a prison, not a market. Our bags were searched,
we were always being watched' (Ana Eugenia). Working conditions had
worsened significantly for the women after the new buildings opened.
Stall rentals had risen as much as 100% in six months from the
beginning of 1979 and the administration began charging for a number
of fictitious additional costs, such as repairs to electricity installations
which were in theory covered by the municipal government.

On 13 September 1979, a group of market women met to form an
association in order to call a halt to the corrupt practices of the market
administration and police and to try to improve their working
conditions. ASUTRAMES drew up a series of demands in a 27-point
petition addressed to the municipal government. The petition included
the following points:

Legal recognition for the Association.
Removal of the present market administration on the grounds of
   corruption.
Removal of all present security personnel.
50% reduction in rates for renting stalls in the markets as of 1 January
   1980.
A subsidized rate for gas, electricity and water.
Offices for the Association and a centre for women market vendors.
Free medical services and nurseries in the main markets.

These demands were simply ignored by the municipal government. The Association then decided to resort to direct action and staged an occupation of the administrative offices of three of the seven markets of San Salvador. In the provincial towns of San Miguel and Santa Ana, the markets were also occupied. The San Salvador Central Market occupation lasted for 12 days, from 11 to 23 December 1979, and a number of hostages from among the administrative personnel were held in the offices. 'During the occupations, the most difficult thing was at night, because they tried to intimidate us. They placed guards outside the markets, who let off gunshots all the time' (Eli, ASUTRAMES member, Mexico City, October 1982).

ASUTRAMES Statement

This is one of the press bulletins issued by ASUTRAMES during the negotiations after the occupations of December 1979:

> ASUTRAMES condemns the reactionary attitude of Mayor Rey Prendes of the PDC. Now that he no longer has us in his hands to manipulate and exploit as he pleases, now that we have an association of market women which defends our interests and fights for the freedom and independence of the market sector, he has tried to suppress our fighting spirit. He tried to impose his puppets as directors of the market administration, men from the PCN, the PDC and ORDEN, in order to neutralize our fight and try to create divisions among us. But ASUTRAMES is not going to permit such a thing to happen but will continue to press for our demands. We carried out a symbolic occupation of the San Miguelito and the Old Barracks markets for four hours in support of our most pressing demands and to show that we are willing to continue the fight whatever the consequences, because Rey Prendes has not kept his promises and we want to see our demands met. Rey Prendes is a political intriguer and a hypocrite who is acting in the interests of the financial oligarchy and Yankee imperialism. He is defending their interests and their economic power, and therefore he is never going to defend us market women. We are not going to accept his word as Mayor as it's nothing but an empty promise but we are determined to remain firm in our fight until we see our demands met. We stress our decision to fight to conquer our most pressing demands whatever the consequences for us.

The press carried out a smear campaign against the market women, claiming they were armed terrorists. However, the market women received enormous popular support and the municipal government was eventually forced to capitulate. The negotiations took place on 20 and 21 December in the offices of the CDHES.

The Association had become well known during the occupations, and its membership increased dramatically. It had been headline news in the press for almost two weeks and had produced a paid television programme to put its point of view across.

The Association found that for the first time the municipal government was taking its demands seriously and was prepared to make concessions which would effectively improve working conditions. However, it was seven months later, after a prolonged rent strike and a number of symbolic occupations, before the municipal government implemented the agreement, lowering the tariffs by 50% and firing the most notorious crooks employed in the market administration.

The Association was given premises in the San Jacinto Market and set about pressing for their other demands. Nursery provisions were given priority and, by the end of 1980, all the main markets of San Salvador had a good day nursery subsidized by the local government. The Association also achieved its demand that the clinics established in the larger markets should give a free service with free medicines. In April 1983, the services had been substantially cut. The Central Market clinic was only open twice a week and, in common with the entire public health service, medicines were almost non-existent.

ASUTRAMES knows that these are partial gains. Affiliated to the FDR in September 1980, the organization has made its position clear – market women will never have a decent life until there is a popular democratic government. The ASUTRAMES offices acquired a small duplicator and reproduced FDR information for distribution in the markets. The organization has participated in the major mass protests over the last three years and has donated food, clothing and time to supporting strikers, political prisoners and other popular causes.

Members of ASUTRAMES have been under constant threat from the security forces and many have been captured, tortured and killed. Ana Eugenia was only 18 years old when she was kidnapped by the National Police:

> ASUTRAMES supported the vigil in the Parque Libertad in San Salvador, which took place after the murder of Mñs Romero. The market women had undertaken to provide coffee and bread to the demonstrators in the park. That's why the Death Squad turned up at the San Jacinto Market on 9 April 1980. They took over an orphanage, a church institution and two schools, all of which are nearby. Then they entered the market. We were in an ASUTRAMES meeting. They beat everyone brutally and captured five people, including myself. I was kidnapped for ten days. They took me to a secret prison and raped me over and over again by forcing the barrel of a gun into me. They demanded information about ASUTRAMES and thousands of other things. The market women saved me. They went to the International Red Cross and the CDHES and got me released.
> Ana Eugenia

Another member of ASUTRAMES explained how the repression increased, until there came a point when the Association had to call a halt to its public activities.

> On 5 September 1981, they captured two young boys, the son and the nephew of a woman who was very well known for her work with ASUTRAMES, Buenaventura Rivas. She had a cheese and cereal stall in the San Jacinto Market. Then at 5 a.m. one morning, the security forces kidnapped her from her house. They took her to her stall in the market, demanding she handed over the arms and propaganda they accused her of storing there. Then they took her away and we knew nothing of her until her body was found eight days later, along with that of her son and two unknown men. The police beat up other women from the market and captured another member of the Association who remains disappeared still. They were after all the most active members, including myself. The police began to search for various people but our security system was very good and we had been warned about what was happening. Every day they came looking for me. I had to abandon the stall, and went into hiding until I could arrange to leave the country secretly. There was nothing else for it.
>
> During the March 1982 elections, the repression increased again. The Association supported abstention and there was a virtual strike in the market. ASUTRAMES gave out leaflets, explaining what the government was trying to do with those 'elections'. It was our last leaflet because afterwards it became too dangerous. A bomb exploded in the San Jacinto Market a little before the election date. Then on 26 March, nine collaborators of the Association were captured. Maria del Carmen Asencio, a great activist and a good friend of mine, was among them. She was captured for the second time and remains disappeared. Then they began following my daughter and she was forced to leave the country as well. She couldn't apply for a passport as she was under age. Her father didn't live with us and I was out of the country, so she had to cross the frontier illegally, swimming the river to get from Guatemala to Mexico.
> Eli, Mexico City, October 1982

Although the organization, in common with so many, has been forced underground, it is still secretly very active in channelling supplies to the controlled zones, where some members have now gone to work.

Notes

1. *El Mundo*, San Salvador, 13 June 1975.
2. 'Testimony of José Antonio Morales Carbonell', Series *Testimonies*, no. 2 (CDHES, Mexico City, June 1982), p. 5.

10 Women for a New Education

I never dreamt that anyone would bother to teach *me* to read and write –
particularly at my age!
60-year-old campesina refugee, León, Nicaragua, participant in an *ANDES
21 de junio* literacy programme, April 1983

Teachers, university professors and students have provided much of the
intellectual leadership for the political organizations in opposition to
the regime. *ANDES 21 de junio* (*Asociación Nacional de Educadores
Salvadoreños*) is a founder member of the BPR and openly expresses its
support for the FDR–FMLN, while both the state and the Catholic
universities have been consistent critics of the lack of democratic and
civil liberties and have argued cogently for the need for social and
economic reforms.

Education has, as a consequence, become a highly charged subject,
with the opposition arguing for greater state expenditure and closer
attention to the needs of the majority of the population, while the
government has shown little concern for improving state facilities and
has repressed dissenting academic opinion. Hundreds of teachers and
academics have been murdered, the UES has been closed down on a
number of occasions by the army and the UCA subjected to bomb
attacks. The Rector of the UES, Felix Ulloa, was killed in 1980. Since the
last closure of the state university, in June 1980, the government has
encouraged the proliferation of private schools and colleges, which
have been given the status of 'university'. These educational institutions
suffer from very poor standards and give tacit or open support to the
oligarchy. Meanwhile, government educational provisions have
deteriorated drastically.

Education has always been a low government spending priority, with
the oligarchy preferring to send their children to private schools and
then universities abroad. In 1979, 56% of the school-age population were
not in school[1] and while figures for illiteracy vary considerably, some
suggest it could be as high as 67%.[2]

Facilities are very poor and particularly in rural areas, the distance to
the nearest school or the cost of educational materials can be prohibitive.
Most important, given the conditions of extreme poverty in which the

71

majority of Salvadorean families live, children are required to work. For these reasons, there is a massive drop-out rate, with only some one-quarter of all pupils registered in the first year finishing their primary education.[3] In 1974, only 18% of the population had completed primary and 3.6% secondary schooling and 0.8% had successfully completed a university degree.[4]

Teachers have been a consistently radical and influential force in El Salvador, where 46% of the population is under the age of 14. Their exceptionally low pay and poor work conditions in part explain their commitment, but teachers, especially in rural areas, where literacy is at a high premium, have functioned as important community leaders.

Women make up over three-quarters of the teaching profession and ANDES estimates that some 90% of its membership is female. The teaching association therefore represents one of the most vocal and important expressions of professional women's organized opposition to the regime.

ANDES claims to represent some 20,000 of the country's 23,000 teachers, although formal membership only reaches 10,000 since open affiliation involves enormous risks. Melida Anaya Montes was the first ANDES General Secretary and later joined the FPL to become Comandante Ana Maria. (Her assassination in Nicaragua in April 1983 has had serious political repercussions which it is beyond the compass of this book to discuss.) The association was founded in 1965 (on 21 June, from which it takes its name), when some 80% of all school teachers staged a demonstration to protest against a new 'Law of Retirements', which increased by one third the period of service necessary to qualify for a pension. This demonstration was the first independent action on the part of a teachers' association; previously, they had been government controlled.

Two years later, in 1967, ANDES was in a position to organize the first general strike by teachers to protest against cuts in the education budget in the name of rationalization. Staggered strikes failed to meet with a response and the Ministry of Education, rather than negotiate, chose to end the school year a month early. At the beginning of the new school year, in February 1968, ANDES held a two-month general strike and occupied the buildings of the ministry – the first time in El Salvador's history that public buildings had been occupied, although this was to become a frequent practice in subsequent years. 'On this occasion, the government suspended negotiations and brought in the troops. Two workers' leaders and a student were killed and hundreds of teachers beaten and imprisoned.'[5] While the government broke the strike, they were unable to destroy the union and were forced to concede it legal recognition.

ANDES staged a second major strike in 1971 which lasted almost as long as the first and received extensive popular backing. In rural areas, ANDES members were established as leaders of the radical opposition to the regime and in the 1972 elections were fundamental in organizing support for the opposition coalition, the UNO.

Convinced of the impossibility of a successful electoral strategy in 1972, because of the levels of repression and fraud, in 1975, ANDES played a key role in the formation of the BPR. From then on, ANDES has worked with the campesino, worker, student and shanty-town sectors in the BPR to help create the mass political opposition which now confronts the regime.

ANDES argues that only through reforms in the social and economic structure of the country, and with an end to the concentration of power in the hands of the oligarchy, can the inadequacies and inequalities of the Salvadorean education system be overcome. It has published a series of devastating reports about the educational situation, highlighting the government's negligence. A national teachers' seminar in 1975 produced an evaluation of the education reforms introduced ten years previously under President Kennedy's Alliance for Progress. ANDES claimed that education, designed for a developed urban society, continued to be the privilege of a narrow elite and irrelevant to the needs of the majority. It criticized the Ministry of Education for failing to take into account the social and economic context of the school-age population, particularly their nutritional and health needs and the job options open to them. They demanded more consultation with teachers, parents and pupils, in order to create more relevant programmes.

Transíto Ramírez worked in the Ministry of Education preparing teachers' materials and was instrumental in drawing up the report:

> The Alliance for Progress reforms were absurd, given the enormous and very basic lack of educational materials available in the majority of state schools. We were preparing television programmes on laboratory work when most teachers counted themselves lucky if there was any chalk available. And more importantly, most rural schools don't have electricity, so the television programmes could only be used in urban areas. The project was very expensive and the money could have been much better spent. Basically, it was a good business deal for the Minister of Education who had shares in the Japanese company which sold the television equipment.
> Los Angeles, December 1982

Under General Romero, ANDES headquarters were raided and then closed down in 1978, and prominent leaders detained. Teachers' houses and school buildings were set on fire or bombed in an attempt to intimidate ANDES members; in the right-wing press, ANDES was accused of fomenting subversion and Communism:

> It was important for us to ensure that parents understood what ANDES' position was, as the mass media was so intent on branding us as Communists in the hands of the Soviets. We held meetings with parents and found their support invaluable. Of course, there were some who had been bought by ORDEN, even secondary school pupils who were members of the

paramilitary groups. On the other hand, there were many brave secondary school students who supported us and formed their own organizations.
Berta, ANDES representative, Nicaragua, May 1983

General Romero's last months in power marked the beginning of a concerted campaign against ANDES members. Prior to 1979, three teachers had been assassinated. In 1979 alone, 33 were murdered:

> We started to receive telephone calls telling us we only had so many hours to live. Then there was a list of teachers' names pinned on the school gate one morning, saying they had been marked out by the death squad. And mock crosses were erected outside the grounds with our names on. We were all terrified.
>
> Elena, ANDES member, Nicaragua, May 1983

School-children were forced to witness the murder of their teachers and, on one particularly macabre occasion, pupils at a rural primary school entered the classroom one day to find their teacher's head on the front desk.

ANDES members have also been attacked during peaceful demonstrations. Maria Luisa de Rojas, General Secretary of the Mejicanos Branch of ANDES, took part in the 8 May 1979 demonstration to protest against the arrest of the General Secretary of the BPR and other leaders:

> There were some 5,000 people on the demonstration, members of the BPR on the whole. We blocked off the main streets of the city centre and staged a sit-in at the Parque Libertad. We sang protest songs and shouted slogans against the government and to demand the release of the BPR leaders and all political prisoners. About mid-day, the National Police moved in and began arresting demonstrators. I suddenly realized that the surrounding buildings were full of soldiers – and then the shooting began. We all tried to flee, rushing towards the Cathedral as it was the only place to go. But only one door was open and everyone was pushing and shoving to get through. They started to use machine guns against the crowd on the Cathedral steps, people were collapsing wounded all about me. Someone shouted: 'Lie down!', and as I threw myself to the ground, I felt a bullet hit me. Others fell on top of me, I never knew if they were alive or dead. After about half an hour, the shooting died down and someone helped me inside the Cathedral. But it was ghastly, thousands of us jammed inside, with the injured moaning in pain all around. It wasn't until 8 p.m. that they let the Red Cross through.
>
> Mexico City, June 1983

After the coup in October 1979, the Ministry of Education was passed to liberal intellectuals. Teachers were promised salary increases and better social security facilities, while the ministry agreed to increase expenditure on education and set up a joint planning agreement with ANDES. ANDES headquarters were returned and the ministry opened a grants programme for the children of the 33 teachers assassinated the previous year. However, these promises proved impossible to fulfil. The mass resignations from the junta in January 1980 included the Minister of Education, Salvador Samayoa. In a televized interview, he announced his resignation and, at the same time, his decision to join the FPL, the armed revolutionary group most strongly connected to the BPR.

Since then, the situation has deteriorated. Teachers' pay is heavily in arrears and members of ANDES have been blacklisted and are unable to find work. The only teacher-training school in the country has been converted into an army barracks, exacerbating the educational crisis. In April 1983, teachers reported that in some areas they had not been paid for four months and 828 schools had been closed down.[6] ANDES reports for the same month that, since 1979, 309 teachers have been murdered, 33 were political prisoners, 24 had disappeared, 4,500 were displaced and some 4,000 in exile.[7]

Despite the repression, ANDES continues to function as a legal organization. If anything, its members have become more radical and new sectors, including school inspectors, technicians and teachers from the private sector have expressed support for ANDES:

> ANDES is not a clandestine organization. We still have our offices and we remain a recognized institution, affiliated to international teachers' associations. The government has tried to make us go underground and treats us just as if we were 'outlaws' but we remain determined to maintain our public protest.
> Berta, ANDES representative, Nicaragua, May 1983

ANDES members are active in the protest against human rights violations and continue their organizational work for the popular organizations. Some are working with the displaced or in the controlled zones, carrying out literacy campaigns and press or political work. In exile, members are involved in solidarity work and are implementing educational and technical training programmes with the refugee communities.

ANDES and Women's Issues

Teaching is one of the few professions open to Salvadorean women and they are well aware of the difficulties that women must face if they wish to receive an education. It is still standard practice to give priority to boys' education, particularly in families where economic resources are scarce, and illiteracy among women is 10% higher than for men.[8] Girls are more likely to suffer from non-attendance, their drop-out rate is higher and they remain the low achievers. It is still not even always acceptable for a woman to become a teacher:

> My parents were campesinos and didn't see why I should continue my education after primary school. But I was determined to carry on and won a full scholarship to the *Escuela Normal*, the teachers' training school. The

75

Mike Goldwater

Guazapa, guerilla controlled territory. Small village school

school offered some 100 of these scholarships to poorer students each year. As my parents didn't like the idea of me going to live in the city on my own, they decided to move with me.

Later, after I had qualified as a teacher and got married, I began to study at the university, teaching at a school during the day. I had two young children whom I left with a child minder nearby. But we lived in a middle-class neighbourhood and I met with a lot of disapproval. Some neighbours would even tell my daughters that I wasn't at home because I was out having a good time with men.
Maria Novoa, Mexico City, February 1983

While the state has made no attempt to erode traditional ideas about women's role in society through the schools, many teachers are aware of the problem:

The great majority of the girls I taught still thought they were born to serve men. When we held activities at the school, the girls would always opt for the 'domestic tasks' and it was difficult to persuade them to take on some other responsibility. They didn't like to put themselves forward but let the boys be the leaders.
Elena, Nicaragua, May 1983

Government textbooks continue to depict women in the 'caring roles' in society and a study carried out in Central American schools clearly showed that a 'lack of aspiration' among young women is related to the limited employment possibilities open to them.[9]

ANDES argues that a new popular education would end discrimination against women in education. In ANDES' work, particularly in the controlled zones and with refugees, it has made a concerted attempt to include women, and its educational materials have been drawn up bearing in mind the need to broaden the context of women's work.

In its union struggles, ANDES achieved parity for women in salary payments and three months maternity leave after the second general strike in 1972. ANDES has criticized the way in which the mass media portray women and in 1975 staged a protest march against the Miss Universe beauty contest held in San Salvador that year. Here ANDES placed emphasis, not so much on the exploitation of women as objects but on the general level of exploitation of Salvadorean women from the poorer classes.

We participated as part of the mass political movement against the exploitation in our country. We opposed the machista attitudes that the beauty contests promoted and argued that women were being used to divert the attention of men and women from the social and economic contradictions of our country.
Juana, ANDES representative, Mexico City, February 1983

A school in a refugee camp — Honduras *Paolo Bosio*

Mealtime in a refugee camp in Honduras *Paolo Bosio*

Notes

1. *Indicadores Económicos y Sociales*, p. 198.

2. J. Ventura, *El Poder Popular en El Salvador* (Salpress and Mex-Sur Editorial S.A., México, 1983), p. 31. The World Bank estimates that in 1971, 30% of the population between the ages of 10 to 25 years and 50% of the population over 25 years were illiterate.

3. In 1975, out of 100 pupils registered in first grade of primary school, 63 were registered in second grade and 26.5% reached sixth grade of primary education. See Guillermo Ungo, 'Fundamentos Socio-Políticos y Fines de la Reforma Educativa', *ECA*, año XXXIII, no. 358 (August 1978).

4. Dunkerley, *The Long War*, p. 69.

5. Phil Gunson, 'Teachers in El Salvador', *Index on Censorship*, vol. 10, no. 2, quoted in: 'El Salvador: Education and Repression', *World University Service* (London, England, October 1981), p. 13.

6. *El Diario de Hoy*, San Salvador, 22 April 1983.

7. *ANDES 21 de junio*, Boletín de la Asociación Nacional de Educadores Salvadoreños (Managua, Nicaragua, April 1983).

8. *The Long War*, p. 69.

9. Ignacio Martín Baro, 'Polarización Social en El Salvador', *ECA*, año XXXVIII, no. 412 (San Salvador, February 1983), pp. 129–42.

Part 3:
In Defiance of Tradition: The Women's Organizations

El Salvador has no history of an organized feminist movement. Women were granted the vote and given equal citizenship for the first time in the 1950 Constitution. While there existed a small women's civil rights organization, the *Liga Femenina Salvadoreña*, whose members were from the incipient middle classes, it could not be described as a broad women's suffrage movement. The League still exists today, a stalwart supporter of the oligarchy, along with a number of women's philanthropic, professional and political organizatiohs. But, as one founder member of the League commented: 'We demanded the right to vote but found that vote to be worthless' (Transíto de Ramírez, Los Angeles, December 1982: Transíto is now in exile and supports the FDR–FMLN. Her daughter, a well-known urban comandante, Lil Milagro Ramírez, has been captured and was last seen in a clandestine prison some three years ago).

Women who have organized around their specific demands all support the political opposition arguing that their oppression as women can only be substantially altered with the overthrow of the present regime. In the 1960s, the Fraternity of Salvadorean Women sought to incorporate women into the political opposition through addressing their specific needs and it has functioned as something of a model for the organizations founded in the late 1970s.

All women's organizations are quick to explain that they are not fighting against men, but with them, for a more just and democratic society. Ideas and opinions about women's issues and the degree of priority they should be given at this stage vary considerably, but it is more than apparent that there are many who now believe that a new society would be incomplete without changes in women's position. The work of the Association of Women of El Salvador (AMES) and other women's organizations in the controlled zones and with refugees has been very impressive in this sense.

The Salvadorean women's organizations which support the FDR–FMLN have not yet formed a united front, although there have been several initiatives in that direction and a growing recognition of the need to do so. The first attempt to form a future national women's organization was the Unified Committee of Salvadorean Women (CUMS), founded in 1982, but internal problems and communication difficulties blocked progress. However, with the creation of further women's organizations, the need to have a unified representation has increased and it is expected that a new co-ordinating body will be founded in the near future.

11 Right-wing Women's Organizations

... Endless afternoon teas when we discussed giving mugs of hot chocolate to needy children at Christmas time or whose turn it was to do the flowers in the Maternity Hospital. Then, suddenly we were discussing what was the best revolver to buy at the weekend, because the campesinos were going Communist again.

Eva, British woman, married into the Salvadorean oligarchy – now divorced, Mexico City, June 1983

The small minority of right-wing women who have formed organizations to support the interests of the oligarchy are primarily ladies of leisure – wives and mothers from the wealthiest sectors of Salvadorean society. Generally middle-aged, they may even have children who are working for the left-wing opposition, but their own closed environment has protected them from any understanding of the reality of their country.

Cameo

They go to mass on Sundays and Holy Days ...
and ring a bell to call for the maid ...
They diet rigorously
and talk on the telephone for six hours a day ...
They play bridge in front of the servants
and speak English ...
They keep money in Swiss banks
and go abroad three times a year ...

They go out on the streets with
bodyguards, grandchildren and cousins
because the fury of the people in arms
threatens the possessions of their heirs ...
and in angry protest
they demand peace and work

They demand that the army restores order ...
The warmongers scream for peace ...

... blood and more blood flows through their coffee plantations

Then
They
Satisfied
Read the memoirs of Henry Kissinger
drink cognac and listen to La Traviata.

Mercedes Durand
Extracts from 'Camafeo' in *A Sangre y Fuego* (Mexico, 1980),
translation, Lyn Geary

They are devout members of the hierarchical Catholic Church, which has been one of the main influences on their lives. It is more common than not for upper-class women to join some religious or philanthropic organization which engages in charity work with the poor, in sharp contrast to the Popular Church's emphasis on self-organization for change. Educational courses run by these religious groups, such as the *Sociedad de Señoras de la Caridad de San Vicente de Paul* (founded 1892), place great emphasis on the need for social integration and obedience to God's will.

There are a variety of professional associations of doctors, nurses and teachers which give tacit support to the regime. None have made statements about the deterioration of conditions in their respective professions or protested against human rights violations. They should be compared with other professional organizations, such as the *National Association of Salvadorean Nurses*, which have published lists of armed incursions into hospitals by the security forces, together with the names of patients, doctors and nurses who have been killed.[1]

Repeating what they hear, women on the right claim that something called 'Salvadorean democracy' is in danger. They never fundamentally question the nature of their political system, which has successfully maintained their small elite in power since the last popular rebellion was put down in 1932. From this viewpoint, the civil war is entirely concerned with the eradication of Communism from their country and the defence of 'liberty'. On human rights, many consider the torture, disappearances, murders and bombings of innocent civilians as unpleasant but absolutely necessary elements of the war. On the other hand, there are those who believe that human rights violations are the work of Communist terrorists, based on information they receive from heavily censored press reports and the Armed Forces Press Commission. They discard other sources, including US congressional hearings and Amnesty International, as Communist propaganda.

Right-wing women have relatives and friends in the army and police forces whose lives are in danger or who have been killed in the civil war. They know their families' business or farming interests have been very hard hit by the political and economic disruptions. In part, they have responded to the crisis by trying to ignore its existence – continuing with the endless round of 'society events'. But they have also rallied to a call to save their privileged world – as women they must protect their children, their families, their religion and, above all, their enormous wealth.

Crusading Women

Like the pots and pan marches in Chile, when right-wing women took to the streets to protest against the Allende Popular Unity government, the ultra-right·in El Salvador has called upon women in times of political emergency. Wives, mothers, daughters of the oligarchy, business women and their lower middle-class employees erupted onto the political scene in a series of well-orchestrated demonstrations against the first junta in late December 1979. While never a crucial factor in the political balance during the exceptionally unstable period after the coup, their participation was an indication of just how polarized Salvadorean society had become and was to provide the right-wing with good moral propaganda material.

In December 1979, two civic organizations were formed, the Crusade for Peace and Work and the Salvadorean Feminine Front. The Crusade successfully united all women to the right of the Christian Democrats, while the Front is unofficially known to be controlled by the ultra-right ARENA Party.

The two December marches by right-wing women were important public relations exercises in support of hardliners in the government. The first took place on 10 December and reportedly some 15,000 women took part, although numbers have been grossly inflated by the local press. The march was headline news: 'Women overcome terrorist attack' and banners calling for 'Peace and Work' and 'Forward Women – the fight is on' were carried by the marchers.

The second march, on 27 December, organized by the Crusade, was calculated to have brought 90,000 men and women onto the streets, although again numbers have been hugely exaggerated. The Crusade was formed shortly after the first march. They published an open letter to the junta expressing their determination to save their fathers, husbands and sons from the international conspiracy threatening their country.[2]

The Crusade received very substantial financial backing for the organization of the march from the right-wing military and political parties. The San Salvador newspapers were filled with alarmist propaganda, calling upon all Salvadorean patriots to halt the terrorist advance and telling women that their families and homes were in danger. The day before, the newspaper *El Mundo* contained eight announcements from the Crusade about the march, including four full-page spreads. Radio and television time was bought for the same

Taking a walk along the street
Banner: We trust our army – We demand more repression
            against the people.
Man: And these bourgeois hags are asking for *peace* and
            work!!!!

purpose. Comments by Archbishop Romero on the Catholic radio station, to the effect that the march did not represent the views of the Salvadorean people and avoided the whole issue of human rights violations, were attacked as a vile calumny on Salvadorean women.[3]

On the day of the march, 'friends and relatives' (*El Mundo*) kindly flew light aircraft and helicopters over San Salvador to protect the demonstration on the route to the staff headquarters of the armed forces. Col. Carranza assured the crowd that the army was doing its utmost to protect property and stated that the government was respecting human rights. His speech was warmly received and the marchers offered their complete support to the armed forces. The march was reported as 'an exemplary show of civic conscience' on the part of Salvadorean women.[4]

The women's civic fronts have virulently opposed US-imposed reforms and in May 1980 staged a demonstration outside the US ambassador's residence. Ambassador Robert White was told to go home, and the women chanted, 'White is red' and 'send White to Cuba'. They have produced a number of published manifestos condemning US congressional interference in El Salvador and adamantly opposing any dialogue with the FDR:

> The Salvadorean people are giving a lesson to the whole world, and especially to the North Americans, because even after almost three years of finding ourselves beset by the guerrilla, a total misgovernment by the PDC and a catastrophic foreign intervention, we still have the moral integrity to continue protesting against such a calamity, financed and encouraged in part by the leftist sectors which have infiltrated the North American government ...
>
> The corruption and moral crisis revealed in the foreign policy of the United States is such that we women raise our voices in protest against the insulting and base behaviour of Mr Christopher Dodd [Democrat Senator], who committed the crass error of calling our country a 'nest of rats' ...
>
> Nicaragua is receiving millions of dollars from the gringos who don't find anything to reproach in the Sandinista totalitarian regime, while, in contrast, they are blocking aid to the Salvadoreans offered by other countries.
>
> It is well known that in the Constituent Assembly, only the women are valiantly defending our sovereignty and protesting against foreign intervention ... Salvadorean women, indignant at such servility and such silence on the part of those with whom we have entrusted the destiny of our Fatherland, demand that all our men declare themselves ready to defend our sovereignty, showing the world that Salvadoreans indeed have dignity.
> Crusade for Peace and Work, July 1982[5]

The Salvadorean Feminine Front pursues much the same line with vitriolic attacks on the United States and the armed forces for imposing a provisional president (Alvaro Magaña) after the March 1982 elections, who was not the ARENA candidate. US Democrat Congressmen, who have sought to limit and condition military and economic aid to El Salvador, have become favourite targets. One full-page statement from the Front had this to say to Clarence Long:

The Democrat Congressman Long has given full rein to his total unworthiness as a man and as a government functionary in his dealings with a country which is a friend to his government and to his nation. Congressman Long thinks to give us alms, kicked towards us with the dirty soles of his shoes, so that the Salvadorean people, on their bended knees, lick them up from the ground with their tongues. Only then will Long feel satisfied and only then will his band of lackeys clap their hands in applause.[6]

ARENA's Women

ARENA is a movement. Its principle cadres are of the middle class, a tiny percentage of Salvadorean society, but educated and vocal. These are not the oligarchs. These are not the politicos and the hacks of the PCN. Many have not participated in politics before. These are the ones who do not have the money to flee to Miami, like the big oligarchs, and their toehold on power and property is profoundly threatened ... They have natural allies in the countryside among the families of ORDEN ... and considerable support among the security forces.[7]

ARENA is guns and slogans. Its political platform is brief: the iron hand against Communism to save private enterprise. Party leader Major D'Aubuisson, termed a 'pathological killer' by US Ambassador Robert White, headed the intelligence division of the National Guard before he was told to resign after the October 1979 coup. He then twice conspired to overthrow the junta, and is unofficially considered to head the paramilitary death squad, the White Warrior Union. ARENA did well in the March 1982 elections. Coming in second behind the PDC's 24 seats, it has 19 members in the Constituent Assembly over which D'Aubuisson now presides.

A surprising number of ARENA voters are female. One ARENA spokesman has even gone so far as to suggest that there are nine to ten women in the party for every man. While women party followers may know little about the history of Nazi Germany, they certainly regard Hitler as a hero and *Mein Kampf* is available in the bookshop of the largest middle-class shopping centre of San Salvador.

ARENA Women's Section Monthly Tea

It was an incongruous event, in many ways reminiscent of an innocent garden party, yet another of the many social occasions with which Salvadorean upper- and middle-class women fill their days. Some 250 people, nearly all women, elegantly dressed and drenched in fine perfumes, had gathered in the garden of the party headquarters where a table had been set up with a lavish display of cakes and blancmange. The perfect hostess, the Women's

---

International Relations Secretary, was at the same time the determined patriot, who told journalists that they were most welcome but on condition they told the TRUTH. The ARENA Party is notorious for its campaign against foreign journalists, who have universally condemned their party leader for his pivotal role in human rights violations.

The political speeches were exceedingly unpleasant. The male Secretary for Workers' Affairs was a clever demagogue who brought his female audience to their feet to applaud Hitler's vision of the Reich, sing the ARENA Party anthem and shout ARENA slogans, such as 'Fatherland yes – Communism no' in a most unladylike fashion.

> We have to save the country. Two systems are confronting us just like 1932. They have co-opted the teachers and are using the pulpits of the Church. We have to protect the right of everyone to build their own private business. We hope that all young women, wives, sisters, daughters, will help us in explaining the dangers of Communism. It's the final challenge. We aren't worried about the elections next year which we will surely win but what does worry us, are the thousand years afterwards. A thousand years of ARENA as the governing party is no false illusion, just as it was no illusion on the part of Hitler to think that the Reich could last for that long.

He felt the party had made a conscious effort to draw women out of their homes and channel their 'anger' to the cause.

ARENA Congressional Deputy, Gloria Salguero Gross, answered a question about women's participation in the party with what amounted to Führer-fervour: 'We women are with our leader – he is our greatest cause, his charisma, his strength, his bravery, his goodness, all offered to us women. Major D'Aubuisson is a true Salvadorean' (San Salvador, April 1983).

Notes

1. See: *ECA*, año XXXV, no. 379 (May 1980), pp. 528–30.
2. *El Mundo*, San Salvador, 18 December 1979.
3. *El Mundo*, San Salvador, 21 December 1979.
4. *El Mundo*, San Salvador, 28 December 1979.
5. 'Dónde esta la dignidad de los salvadoreños?, Cruzada Pro-Paz y Trabajo', *ECA*, año XXXVII, no. 405 (July 1982), pp. 749–50.
6. *Diario de Hoy*, San Salvador, 26 April 1983.
7. 'El Salvador – Beyond Elections', *NACLA*, vol. XVI, no. 2 (March–April 1982), p. 16.

12 Women Organizing for Change

The Fraternity of Salvadorean Women 1957–69

The Fraternity of Salvadorean Women (FMS) was formed in 1957 by a group of four women. The organization was set up under the influence of the Salvadorean Communist Party, but accepted members who were not affiliated. It was the only organization of the day concerned for women's rights. As one working-class member of FMS recalled: 'the other women's organizations only met to play poker, canasta and generally show off' (Frida, interview with AMES, Mexico, June 1982).[1]

The statutes of the FMS outlined the following platform:

Organize campesina women to gain their rights.
Right to social security and Labour Code for protection for domestic workers.
Equal pay for equal work.
Nurseries for working mothers.
Halt to petty extortion against market women.
Working-class housing.
More schools and recreation centres.

Despite its very small membership at the start, the FMS soon grew to well over 1,000 members, with branches in most regions of the country:

The most receptive sectors were the market women and factory workers. We visited women to talk about their situation. We would go to the markets and made a particular impact there. So when the market women sold their products, they would make a habit of slipping one of our leaflets into the bag of goods. The setting up of our branch in Sonsonate was a great occasion for us. I got up on a bench in the middle of the market and we were soon surrounded. I spoke of the need to organize, that an individual alone cannot change things. I said we had to fight for improvements, such as a proper building for the market and a nursery for their children. After we had spoken, the women in the market restaurants invited us to eat with them and that was how the Sonsonate branch was born.

But many men resented women's participation in the Fraternity. I knew party comrades and trade union leaders with terribly traditional attitudes. Revolutionaries in public and feudal lords at home, as the saying goes. Men who were renowned working-class leaders but would beat up their wives if they got in late from one of our meetings.
Liliam Jiménez, founding member of the FMS, March 1983, Mexico City

Liliam Jiménez also helped found the Union of Guatemalan Women during the period of the reform-minded governments of Arévalo and Arbenz (1950–4). After the US-backed coup against Arbenz, Liliam was forced to leave Guatemala and return to El Salvador, working as a teacher and with the FMS. Liliam was again forced into exile in 1961 after she received death threats. Her strong commitment to women's rights led her to write the first Salvadorean publication on the oppression of women, *The Condition of Women in El Salvador*, published in Mexico in 1961. The book was embargoed in El Salvador.

The FMS carried out a number of cultural, educational and political activities and also produced a monthly magazine called *Fraternity*. They opened a centre for their activities in San Salvador, with a school for members' children, and gave sewing and secretarial classes. They also organized meetings and demonstrations in support of trade unionists on strike and in aid of political prisoners:

We helped as best we could. Sometimes even in fights, throwing stones and other things against the security forces who came to break up the picket lines or arrest the trade union leaders. When our Party Secretary General, Salvador Cayetano Carpio, started a hunger strike for a wage rise for the bakers we helped out. We kept guard against the security forces and helped in the communal kitchen which was set up for the support committee.
Liliam Jiménez

The FMS was active in the protest movement which brought down the Lemus regime (1956–60) but, in common with many other groups, it became progressively disillusioned by the perpetual electoral frauds. In 1967, a progressive candidate, backed by the Communist Party, won the elections, but again the military fraudulently imposed their own candidate. The PCS split, with Salvador Cayetano Carpio opting for armed struggle. The repression against members of the party, the trade union movement and other progressive organizations increased. The FMS also suffered. Members such as Fidelina Raymundo were imprisoned, and others decided to join the new armed movement. The Fraternity was disbanded, but many of its ideas and methods have been taken up by the new women's organizations formed in the 1970s.

The Association of Women of El Salvador (AMES)

The Association of Women of El Salvador (founded in 1979), is the largest of the women's organizations which support the FDR–FMLN:

> AMES is a channel for the incorporation of those sectors of women who, on account of their specific conditions (housewives, professionals, some teachers, slum-dwellers and students) have not yet been incorporated into the popular struggle.[2]

As Maria Luisa de Rojas, one of the founding members of AMES explained, many women are frightened of joining an overtly political organization but are prepared to organize with other women around issues which affect them immediately.

Since its foundation, AMES has been transformed from a small mainly middle-class group to a large popular-based organization, with an increasingly clear and more elaborate analysis of women's specific oppression.

> We first tried to found the Association in 1978. There were only four women at the time but we all believed firmly in the need to organize women. We were greatly influenced by the work of the FMS and some of us had collaborated with that organization back in 1968 during the teachers' massive strike. So we founded AMES, but the repression soon put a stop to this first attempt. I was wounded in a demonstration and had to retire from political activities for a while to recuperate and another member was killed in the massacre, when the security forces dislodged the peaceful occupation of the Venezuelan Embassy.
>
> It was slightly over a year later when we felt that conditions were suitable for another attempt. This time there were intially only five of us, but we began to visit women we knew to be active in their local Christian communities. While some felt frightened about participating in an organization which was not related to the church, others were very enthusiastic. We soon began to grow in numbers and in September 1979, we organized our foundation congress. For New Year, we held a cultural act with some 60 women present. By then, we felt sufficiently established to begin work with women in the poorest districts of San Salvador. We founded the Women's Neighbourhood Committees which still exist today. In July 1980, AMES staged its first public demonstration, when the El Calvario church was occupied for a few hours to demand a reduction in the price of basic food stuffs. The church is near the Central Market and so, with our microphones, shoppers could hear our demands and many came up to show their support. AMES began to win recognition as an organization, fighting for the interests of women from the exploited classes.
> Maria Luisa de Rojas, July 1983, Mexico City

The AMES leadership stresses that at this moment:

> our fundamental demands are those of the people, that's to say, the exploited classes. Women are taking part in the struggle because our vital interests, survival and the development of our nation, are the same as those of men. The main enemy of both men and women in El Salvador is imperialism, the oligarchy and the military governments. We believe that men and women together must free ourselves so as to be able to construct a new form of

95

society. And for this reason we have expressed our support for the Programme of the Revolutionary Democratic Government of the FMLN–FDR.[3]

However, for AMES, this does not imply that the questions concerning women's position in society should be avoided until the FDR–FMLN takes power. AMES wishes to see the FDR–FMLN adopt a 'Minimum Women's Programme' as part of its published manifesto and believes that as far as conditions permit, it is necessary to work for change now.

We are a group with a specific condition and specific demands and we cannot wait for socialism and structural changes to solve the problems tomorrow, which today are the cause of our limitations ...

A woman's decision to become a political activist implies a much longer and more difficult process than that taken by a man. Obviously this does not signify that we have resolved our specific problem of 'being women' nor that militancy can be the panacea which allows us to find our own identity. However, we think that the characteristic of a 'revolutionary feminism' is that it is part of a project for the transformation of society. We also know that the liberation of women requires a level of collective consciousness which in turn is the product of a new ideological development.[4]

AMES and Family Planning

Few women in AMES have taken the issue of women's liberation further than the question of equal opportunity and shared responsibility for domestic work and child-care. However, AMES does stress the importance of sexual education and believes it is a step towards better, more permanent relationships between couples. In their talks, they emphasize the need to make men more responsible towards their children in order to strengthen the family. While AMES criticizes the authoritarian nature of the family as it exists today, they believe it is possible to transform it into an egalitarian social unit.

AMES is more cautious on issues such as birth control and the prevention of unwanted pregnancies, in part because of the influence of the Catholic Church at an individual level, though AMES has no direct connection with the church. They criticize both the aims and the methods of state family planning programmes, arguing, in common with the Popular Church, that they are designed to control the poor, not to help them. AMES states that women are being denied their 'right to maternity', or the right to choose whether or not to be a mother.

AMES has no official position on family planning or abortion. In part this is because of priorities: there are other more urgent necessities for Salvadorean women, above all, an end to the civilian massacres and national liberation. But it is also because

---

AMES has a democratic and integrated concept of society. We wish to see a complete women's programme implemented, but first it is absolutely necessary to embark upon a huge amount of educational work. We cannot impose a programme from above without prior consultation or without consideration for the cultural traditions of the vast majority of the Salvadorean population. And while AMES has begun such educational work, especially among refugees and in the controlled zones, we cannot hope to make serious progress until the war has ended.

AMES members in Mexico, or Costa Rica tend to be more open on such issues as family planning and the termination of unwanted pregnancies, but it is still more common than not for women to consider that, at the present time, the revolution needs its children. Personally, I believe that both men and women should be given sexual education from the fourth grade of primary school, so that when women reach the age of sexual maturity, they may enjoy their body as they consider suitable but their sexuality should be expressed within the continuous life of a couple. Women should be allowed to determine the number of children they wish to have, on the basis of their capacity to attend to them emotionally and economically. I also believe that women should be given the right to obtain an abortion through state health facilities, but it is a very sensitive issue and my views are not shared by many.

Maria Novoa, AMES, Mexico City, July 1983

To prevent women from being relegated to a secondary role, AMES suggests:

... even after the Revolutionary Democratic Government is constituted, we will have to continue to fight against the traditional attitudes of men and women. The evils of the system of exploitation and oppression will continue to exist for some time, mainly in those areas which concern women; it is impossible for them to disappear from one day to the next.[5]

AMES has been involved in important educational work and has published a number of pamphlets on the social and working conditions of women, within a general analysis of their double oppression.

In 1980, AMES began to form the Women's Neighbourhood Committees in the poorest districts of San Salvador. They were to prove remarkably successful:

The idea of the Committees was to organize women around their immediate needs – the lack of basic services, particularly water and electricity. We would hold a meeting of women from a certain neighbourhood to discuss their needs and then we would help with the necessary work of filing a request for services at the Town Hall. Or even, when it was apparent that we were not going to get anywhere with the local government, the whole neighbourhood

97

Woman combatant   *from an AMES poster*

would get together on a Sunday to work putting in the drains or paving the streets. If it was hard physical work, the men would do it while the women prepared a meal for everyone. Also, when there was a price rise, the Committees would produce leaflets in protest, demanding subsidies for basic goods. Through this kind of work, women became more and more politically conscious and began to participate in solidarity work with other sectors. Whenever there was a march or protest against human rights violations, the Committees would be there.
Maria Luisa de Rojas

> ... when a woman says
> that gender is a political category
> she can begin to stop being woman in herself
> to become woman for herself
> construct a woman as a woman
> part of humanity
> and not of her gender ...
>
> Roque Dalton
> Association of Women of El Salvador
> Translation: Lyn Geary

Because of political conditions, the type of organizational work AMES was able to undertake in the cities was increasingly restricted. AMES members worked in co-operative workshops and assisted in human rights work, collecting medicine and clothing. In the internal refugee camps, they helped in nursery care and literacy programmes.

AMES has recently suffered from severe internal divisions and their international work has been affected as a consequence. On the other hand, in the controlled zones, their work has grown significantly.

The Association of Progressive Women of El Salvador (AMPES)

AMPES was first founded in 1975, during the International Year of Women, and is a member of the International Democratic Federation of Women. It claims the most direct continuity with the FMS and some of the founder members of the Fraternity are today working in AMPES.

AMPES initially concentrated its attention on women workers and collaborated with the PCS trade unions:

> AMPES' work was basically to try and get more women to join the trade unions and political organizations. We organized women around their own demands, such as work conditions, the lack of nurseries. We also tried to work with housewives, usually the wives of trade unionists. In 1977, we drew up a petition in the name of AMPES which was distributed to factory owners. As a result, a few agreed to install nurseries.
> When the United Trade Union Committee (CUTS) was formed, they established the post of Secretary of Women's Affairs and so we didn't

ASOCIACION
DE
MUJERES
PROGRESISTAS
DE
EL SALVADOR

**Miembro del Comité de Unidad de Mujeres
Salvadoreñas
Apartado Postal:**

★ AMPES ★

Explanatory Pamphlet on the Aims of the Association of Progressive
Women of El Salvador.

continue the work of AMPES. Then, in 1978, the offices of the CUTS were bombed. We had to end our open activities and work secretly. Many women from AMPES decided to go to the combat zones, or were forced to leave the country.

In 1981, AMPES was refounded but this time in the controlled zones. It was felt necessary to organize women in the fronts and also, through contacts with women who were sympathetic to the organization previously, we created a network of messengers in Guazapa, Suchitoto and San Salvador, which is functioning very efficiently.

In December 1981, the Sylvia Battalion was formed, comprising women organized in AMPES. Women are gaining new experiences which will help the national organization of women we all want to see formed, when we have a popular democratic government.

Sonia, representative of AMPES, Mexico DF, June 1983

The Unified Committee of Salvadorean Women (CUMS)

The Unified Committee of Salvadorean Women (CUMS) was a long-standing project of the different women's organizations. It was first proposed in October 1981 by a number of the mass organizations, through their women members in exile in Costa Rica, and a draft 'Letter of Principles' drawn up.

The CUMS celebrated its first local congress in October 1982 and drew up an organizational structure to give equal representation to all the organizations of women which wished to participate.

We feel greatly strengthened by the knowledge that women from the different revolutionary organizations have been able to come together and agree on certain basic principles about what we, as women, are fighting for.

At the moment our work is primarily consciousness raising. With the civil war as it stands, there is no point in fighting the government on a legal basis. Anyway, apart from a few discrepancies, the legal position of women in El Salvador is pretty good. The problem is, as with all Salvadorean laws, it's water off a duck's back. Just as all the trade union laws are ignored, women's rights are just the paper they're written on. We are trying to get Salvadorean women to start asking questions about the role society has traditionally assigned them. In our discussion groups, we talk about women's double exploitation and a bit about the political history of El Salvador and the revolutionary organizations. We explain the importance of unity in front of a common enemy. I like to explain the need for unity in terms of a heavy sack which has to be lifted. Everyone has their own ideas about how it should be done, but if everyone agrees to lift it together, it suddenly becomes a very easy task.

We have learnt a lot from the Nicaraguan experience and as far as the 'woman question' is concerned, we hope to go a bit further. We have had time to experiment and to think. But we are all concerned about what will happen after the revolution. The socialization of child-care and domestic work is no easy matter and above all, it costs money – nurseries, school meals, etc. And

we don't suppose that the United States will continue to be so generous with its aid, once the FDR takes power!
Irene, Public Relations Commission, CUMS, Nicaragua, May 1983

However, the difficulties of organizing a unified committee, both in El Salvador and the different Central American countries, proved too great. Communications within El Salvador between the women's organizations were difficult to maintain and the exiled representatives too dispersed throughout Central America and Europe.

The CUMS has retained its name but now functions mainly as a women refugee co-ordinating body, particularly in Mexico and Nicaragua.

The Association of Salvadorean Women (ASMUSA)

The Association of Salvadorean Women (ASMUSA) was founded on 27 August 1983 in the controlled zones of Guazapa by 47 women combatants and women members of the popular mass organizations. It is therefore one of the most recently established women's organizations. The women in the controlled zones wished to organize to fight for the right to participate in production and defence work on an equal basis with men. They demanded child-care provisions and greater co-operation from men in domestic work.

> We began working with the campesino co-operative, *Unión Nacional de Comunidades del Frente para la Liberación* (UNACOFL) and the Health Brigade 'Manuel Federico Castillo'. ASMUSA organized literacy and primary school classes as well as talks on health, maternity and child-care for the women of the co-operative and women were incorporated into the health brigade for the first time. We now have several nurseries in operation although resources are very poor.
>
> We have formed active ASMUSA groups in other areas, including Cerro San Pedro, Usulután, San Augustín and Sonocosta and our representatives meet on a regular basis to co-ordinate work. We also have representatives in Nicaragua, Mexico and Costa Rica whose main activities are to fund raise and publish information on the situation of women in El Salvador. We have organized handicraft and sewing workshops for women refugees as well.
>
> An essential part of our work is to discuss the changing role of women. We believe that both men and women must work together to change their attitudes. We are not against men, as some feminists seem to be. We feel that women should formulate their demands now and when we have a true democratic government in El Salvador, these demands will be respected.
> Lilian, ASMUSA representative, Mexico City, November 1983

Postscript on the Women's Organizations

In July 1984, a new initiative to form a national women's organization aligned to the FDR was launched. At a conference of Salvadorean women's organizations, it was agreed to set up a Constitutive Committee with a view to creating a Federation of Salvadorean Women.

The conference brought together the largest number of women's organizations to date and included representatives from the following women's organizations:

the Association of Women of El Salvador
the Association of Progressive Women of El Salvador (AMPES)
the Association of Salvadorean Women – Lil Milagro Ramírez (AMS–LMR)
the Association of Salvadorean Women (ASMUSA)
the Unified Committee of Salvadorean Women (CUMS)
the Organization of Salvadorean Women (ORMUSA)

The Statement of Principles and Objectives of the Federation was drawn up at the conference and signed by all the organizations present at the conference (see Annex). The women's organizations are now confident that a unified representative body will be formed and that as a consequence, both their work to incorporate more women into the movement for social justice and a popular democratic government and their work in favour of women's rights will be greatly strengthened.

Members of the Constitutive Committee have already represented the new Federation at a number of international meetings of women, including the Non-Government Organizations Conference of Women at Nairobi in July 1985.

Notes

1. We would like to thank Maria Novoa, AMES representative in Mexico, for kindly giving us the opportunity to listen to this interview.
2. AMES: 'Participación de la Mujer Latinoamericana en las Organizaciones Sociales y Políticas – reflexiones de las mujeres salvadoreñas', paper presented at the first Latin American Seminar on Research on Women, San José, Costa Rica (8–14 November 1981), p. 10.
3. AMES, 'Desde los Frentes' (Mexico D.F., 1983), p. 20.
4. 'Participación de la Mujer Latinoamericana', pp. 11–12.
5. *Boletín Internacional AMES* (a newsletter, issued intermittently), año 2, no. 2 (San José, Costa Rica), p. 13.

13 Women, Political Prisoners and Refugees

The Women's Section of the Committee of Political Prisoners of El Salvador (COPPES)

The political prisoners in the Women's Prison on the outskirts of San Salvador have shown enormous resilience despite their very difficult situation. They have organized a powerful and disciplined committee which has won a number of major concessions from the prison authorities and which, with the help of the Committee of Mothers and other human rights organizations, has kept the existence of political prisoners in the public eye, to the discomfort of the government.

The military regimes in power have never been averse to arresting leaders of the political opposition, but only in recent years has this become a systematic practice. While most political prisoners have been involved in trade union or political work, there are also cases of people who have been picked up on suspicion and who have had no history of participation in any organization.

There is very little apparent logic in the selection of people who are sent to state prisons as opposed to being killed or kept in a clandestine prison. Some 'disappeared' prisoners are transferred because there has been much publicity about their capture, but this is by no means always the case. Most prisoners are badly tortured and forced to sign unread 'confessions' before they are passed to the state prison.

Nearly all the political prisoners are detained without charges and never brought to trial. Under Decree 507, all normal legal proceedings have been suspended and trials are, in theory, conducted in closed sessions by a military tribunal. A defence lawyer may not be brought in until a period of six months has elapsed. However, in practice, trials rarely take place.

> After two months in prison, I heard the first news about why I was being held as a political prisoner. A military judge came to see me and read out the charges – I had been accused of stealing a car. He then announced that the courts had found me innocent and therefore I would shortly be released. I remained in prison another two years until the government graciously let me

out under the amnesty in May 1983. My poor parents spent those two years in the Ministry of Justice and the Supreme Court.
Marbel, Mexico City, June 1983

The released prisoners all feared for their lives. Most received political asylum in other countries, but others were killed by the security forces. The amnesty was largely a public relations exercise, designed to show that the Salvadorean government was serious about its promise to improve human rights; new prisoners soon took their place. It was also hoped that the amnesty would defuse the growing militancy of the COPPES committees and their support network.

COPPES was first formed in September 1980 in the two men's prisons which held political prisoners and in the Women's Prison at Ilopango. At that time, there were 22 women political prisoners who were held in a separate block from the common prisoners, but the number expanded very rapidly:

> The political prisoners' section is a three-storey building with access to a small patio. Downstairs, there's a small kitchen and a common room. Upstairs, on each floor there is one dormitory, each with 30 beds and the bedrooms for the wardens. By the time I was released we were very overcrowded – over 90 of us with 10 children as well. We had to take it in turns to sleep on the floor.
> Marbel

The main aim of COPPES is to win the release of the political prisoners and to call a halt to the harassment and frequent detention of their visitors. They also denounce the government and support the FDR–FMLN in every way they can.

COPPES functions as the elected representative body of all the political prisoners. It has shown what organized action can achieve and, in comparison to the situation of the common prisoners, has won a surprising degree of autonomy. Over the last three years, it has staged a number of hunger strikes and occupations of the administrative offices of the prison and sent out bulletins which have received wide distribution in El Salvador and abroad. It has also managed to improve political prisoners' living conditions. Equally, it now supervises discipline within the building. The Committee arranges the daily timetables, ensuring that all women are in the building by 8 p.m. and in their bedrooms with the lights out at 10 p.m. To prevent security forces from entering their bedrooms, they lock themselves in with padlocks they have saved up to buy. All disciplinary problems are brought before the Committee and the two prison wardens previously assigned these duties no longer perform them. COPPES prepares the prison food in its own kitchen which has a stove provided by the Red Cross for this purpose. There is a special commission which organizes the daily menu, using the prison food stocks, invariably rice and beans, together with additional food brought in by prisoners' relatives and solidarity groups. In this way, all food is shared communally. The women regard this as one of the great triumphs of COPPES, as previously the food was of very low nutritive value and unhygienically prepared, the source of continuous gastro-entiritic disorders. However, prisoners remain heavily dependent on what visitors bring in for them, as the prison budget allows about US 10 cents a day per person.

COPPES has also undertaken educational and social activities. The revolutionary radio stations are monitored daily and brief news bulletins circulated among the prisoners. COPPES has set up a mural newspaper, in defiance of the prison authorities, which comments on the national political situation.

The two major problems which COPPES must confront daily are the very poor health conditions of the majority of the prisoners and the constant fear of harassment by the security forces. Most women who arrive at the prison have been subjected to brutal torture and a prolonged stay in a secret prison. They arrive in a very weak condition from which many are unable to recover because of the inadequate food and health facilities. Two doctors visit the prison, but they are very negligent, in part, as one prisoner explained, because their pay is always in arrears. COPPES won its demand to have a specialized gynaecologist attend the prisoners, many of whom have suffered from multiple rapes by the security forces with obvious consequences. But medicines are not available through the prison and have to be brought in by visitors.

The guards in and around the prison deliberately provoke the political prisoners. Many guards are members of the death squads and openly discuss their activities in loud voices. They also insinuate that relatives of the prisoners are on their lists. Although the women prisoners have not been subjected to the brutal beatings and searches which have taken place in the men's prisons, they have been taken to the National Police headquarters for interrogation under torture. In June 1983, for the first time, the prison guards entered the political section and ransacked the building, taking away personal possessions and a television set which had been bought jointly by the women. It is feared that this may prove the beginning of further repressive measures.

The most prolonged hunger strike organized by COPPES was timed to coincide with the Pope's visit to El Salvador, in February 1983. Women and men participated. In the Women's Prison, 18 prisoners went on strike for 32 days to demand the liberty of all political prisoners and the end to human rights violations. As a consequence some have suffered irreversible damage to their health. After the strike 14 women and 2 children were released.

The work of COPPES is but a small indication of the determination and resolve of the women prisoners to demand respect for their human rights. Despite their exceptionally disheartening conditions, they have protested using all the means at their disposal and have carried out educational and political activities designed to support the work of the FDR–FMLN:

We called COPPES 'another barricade for the revolution'. It's true, we were an enclave of revolutionary supporters. Before I was captured, I hadn't participated in any organization, but the experience of being a political prisoner soon changes your mind. Through COPPES I learnt a lot about the political situation of our country and understood the need for an armed struggle against our dictatorship. And I learnt how we could organize to improve our conditions through sharing as a community. Now I've been released and forced into exile, but you can't forget all those people you have left behind suffering in prison. I'm now working in the Committee of Relatives of the Disappeared and Political Prisoners.
Marbel

The Committees of Mothers and Relatives of the Disappeared, Assassinated and Political Prisoners

The 'mothers', as they are generally referred to, are women who until a few years ago had never spoken in public, never organized a campaign. Many, like Hilda for example, come from very poor campesino backgrounds and can barely write their names. Hilda left her country for the first time at the age of 63 to talk to human rights organizations, politicians and solidarity groups. It was difficult, she explained, but then she had to do it. Two of her sons had been killed in 1980 and the other disappeared in 1981.

The mothers put their own individual tragedies in a broader context. They support the FDR–FMLN on a negotiated solution, condemn the role of the United States and have opted for electoral abstention on the grounds that their children have been denied the vote and that therefore the conditions for free elections do not exist.

Vilma Cruz – Member of the Committee of Mothers, Monseñor Oscar Arnulfo Romero

After the triumph . . . I want freedom, freedom to be able to walk in the streets, shout if I feel like it, run and shout in the streets. What I mean is not to have to think about security measures all the time and not feel so nervous.

Vilma was about 40 years old, tall and gawkily thin. She had lank hair, cut well above her shoulders and thick-rimmed spectacles. She had not contributed much to the discussion about the committee and its work, but when asked about her life had suddenly become very animated. She fished in her bag for her pills for her weak heart and migraine headaches:

I suffer from nerves a lot. At the moment I'm taking seven

---

different types of medicine. When I'm really bad, I have to take 500 mg of one medicine every four hours. I start to tremble uncontrollably and feel dizzy or have terrible headaches. And sometimes, in the street, I forget where I am. I don't know whether it's Mexico or El Salvador or what I'm meant to be doing. Just don't remember.

She began to talk about her family:

40 soldiers rushed into the house and seized him – my son. They pushed him onto the ground and beat him with their guns, over and over again, while they held me so I could do nothing but watch. They broke his arm and he now has three fingers which are useless. And then they took him away. They didn't kill him, thank the Lord!

Instead he was taken from our farm in Suchitoto to the National Police in San Salvador and kept detained for 46 days. Marianella García-Villas from the Human Rights helped to get him out. They denied that he was there, said I was mistaken and that he had just left home. It's the rule that you can take clean clothes to prisoners and they hand you over the dirty ones. So to try and prove he was there, I looked out some old clothes which I didn't mind losing and on the Saturday, I went to the prison and handed them in. The clothes he had on when he was captured were returned to me. So then I went back to the police authorities with Roberto's clothes and asked them how they could go on denying that he was in prison. And we got him out. That was back in 1978 and he was captured and detained for a short period in 1981 – 14 March 1981. And they killed one of my sisters, Emilia Delmi González on 29 September 1980 and the next day I had to go and officially recognize the body of my cousin, Héctor Antonio, because there was no one else to do it. His body was riddled with bullets – 22 bullets they said in the report. My family has suffered terribly from the repression. Some of my cousins' families have all been murdered. I don't know whether my brothers and sisters are still alive. Emilia is dead but I have three other sisters and no way of knowing what has happened to them. They've been on the hunt for my eldest brother, Lorenzo, since way back. My father's ranch in Suchitoto has been searched countless times. He used to have to go and sleep out in the hills when the army or the National Guard were reported in the area. Now he says he is too old to go on living like that and if they want to get him, he's not going to do anything to avoid it. 'I need to sleep in my bed at night now', he told me the last time I saw him. He became a wanted man after my husband was killed in 1974 by the National Guard. They shot four bullets into my husband's back and beat his arms and his face terribly. We lived in Zacatecoluca and he had been active in organizing a co-operative on a cotton plantation.

Vilma paused for a minute and then added:

It's not like the United States thinks. We want a juster society, education for our children, an end to the terrible poverty and to live without fear. I'm in the Committee because I couldn't support the memory of my dead relatives, without doing what I can to stop the repression. My nerves were very bad yesterday. I got a bad spell of dizziness in the street. But I had to come into the Committee office and that always makes me feel better ...

Mexico City, January 1983

The *Comité de Madres y Familiares de Presos, Desaparecidos y Asesinados Políticos de El Salvador, Monseñor Oscar Arnulfo Romero* was founded in 1977 by 12 mothers at a Christmas Eve supper offered to them by the late Archbishop. Since then, the Committee has been remarkably active and has staged a number of public vigils and occupations of buildings.

In 1978 members of the Committee staged their first hunger strike, followed by a three-month occupation of the Red Cross offices in San Salvador to demand the release of all political prisoners. After the coup of October 1979, the mothers spoke on a number of occasions to the government but to no avail. A year later, in October 1980, after they had been dislodged from a public vigil in the main square of San Salvador, they occupied the offices of the Ministry of Justice. They were forcibly removed by the National Guard a week later. In the following year they staged a number of occupations of churches, but even that avenue of protest was closed to them in the end, because it became too dangerous. The death squad published a statement claiming they would cut off the head of every Committee member. One mother was killed and a number captured or disappeared.

There are some 400 mothers who have openly affiliated to the Committee despite the risks involved. In San Salvador, the Committee headquarters is a table under the shelter of three mango trees in the garden of the Archbishopric. Their files are kept in the garden shed where the CDHES has its offices but when it rains, there is no alternative but to close up shop.

Much of their daily life takes place around this 'office'. The garden tap has been converted into a washing area and they prepare lunch for themselves and the human rights workers on a couple of charcoal stoves. The younger children are kept out of harm's way in a hammock slung between two of the mango trees and the older children entertain themselves in the grounds. In part, the mothers need the emotional support that such a communal life-style can bring but on the other hand, many simply do not have anywhere else they can safely go. Carmen has spent two years in San Salvador, forced to leave her farm in Chalatenango because of the army's scorched earth policies. Her house had been razed to the ground and her husband killed. With her son imprisoned, she fears for her life and that of her three other children. She lives moving from house to house to keep the security forces off her tracks. 'Now my home is here with the Committee', she explained.

Another committee, CODEFAM (*Comité de Familiares Pro-Libertad de Presos, Desaparecidos Políticos de El Salvador*), was founded in September 1981. When Marianella García-Villas was murdered in March 1983, the Committee was named after her.

CODEFAM has been given time on the church radio station and thus has the opportunity to denounce human rights violations daily:

> The radio programme is very useful because the church station is widely listened to. For instance, when the political prisoners staged their hunger strike during the Pope's visit, we broadcast their demands. And recently in April, when two young girls from one of the refugee camps in San Salvador were captured, we put their names across on the programme every day until they were eventually transferred from a secret prison to the Women's Prison. We regard it as a triumph to have got them into a public prison, although they are minors, and now we are demanding their release. Of course we exhaust all the legal channels as well but these days we just think of it as a formality. There have been occasions when we have presented a Habeas Corpus petition to the Supreme Court of Justice and the official concerned has simply torn the paper up in front of us and told us to get out.
>
> Sara, CODEFAM, San Salvador, April 1983

Members in exile have set up committees in Mexico City to carry out the solidarity work they cannot undertake in El Salvador because of the political repression. They have made an enormous impact both in El Salvador and abroad. It is impossible to forget these mothers and the matter-of-fact way in which they relate their experiences, an indication that they know their suffering is by no means unique.

Women's Organizations and Refugees

> 15 army trucks arrived and the soldiers set up an ambush to try and kill us all. We managed to flee across the river and up into the hills. We hid for three days and nights with nothing to eat. Then one of my sons went down into the village to see if the army had left. He came back to tell us that they had destroyed everything, that they had taken all the maize, all the cows and had burnt every house in sight. They had left nothing, absolutely nothing. We took shelter with a campesino family for a while, but then we heard that the army was back in the area. We had to flee to the church refuge here. But if that man Reagan wasn't sending bullets to the army, we wouldn't be in this situation.
>
> Carmen, 60-year-old campesina from Chalatenango, church refuge, San Salvador, April 1983

There are no exact figures for the numbers of Salvadoreans who have been forced to leave their homes because of the civil war. Some are economic refugees, but the great majority have fled because of the repression. The CDHES estimates that there are now more than 500,000 displaced persons who have moved to areas away from the conflict zones and some 1 million (20% of the entire population) living outside the country. The vast majority of these displaced and refugees are women, children and old people.

The living conditions of the displaced are invariably extremely difficult and many must rely on church and humanitarian organizations for basic assistance. While the Catholic Church does its best and has set up a number of camps and refuges, particularly in San Salvador, these cannot meet the demand and are very overcrowded: their inadequate sanitation and water facilities create enormous health hazards. There are 300 displaced people crowded into the crypt of the San Roque Church and some 900 living on the sports field of the San José de la Montaña seminary in San Salvador. The Salvadorean government has done little to aid the displaced, choosing instead to see them as potential subversives who must be carefully watched. The security forces have raided the camps, captured community leaders and stolen possessions and church supplies. The majority of the displaced are therefore reluctant to leave the camps and prefer what little protection the church can offer.

In Honduras, conditions are equally difficult. The approximately 32,000 campesino refugees (75% women and children) from the bordering departments of El Salvador have been herded into prison-like camps to which access has been severely restricted. These refugees have been moved away from the border to facilitate military operations and now must endure life on the barren and wind-swept interior plateau. Many have spent up to three years as refugees and nearly all have been forced to flee from Salvadorean army and air force attacks on their homes. At least 2,000 refugees and probably many more have been massacred in joint operations by the two armies while trying to flee across the border. Both Salvadorean and Honduras security forces have raided the camps and refugees and community workers have been badly beaten up or even killed.[1]

The women's organizations have not been able to work with the communities of displaced people in El Salvador, nor with refugees in Honduras or Guatemala, for fear of reprisals. However, they are organizing women refugees in the Central American countries where they have been allowed to set up representations and in Mexico and the US. Within their limited means, they provide community services, education programmes and support small workshop projects. The women's organizations are also an important source of information for many refugees who would otherwise be isolated from events in their country and a channel by means of which they can express support for the revolutionary movement:

In Mexico City, we believe there are some 150,000 refugees. The great majority are illegal, fear deportation and live in very precarious economic circumstances. They can't register their children at schools or use the Mexican health system for fear of detection. So they have to rely on self-help projects. We have established two small primary schools and a number of –very modest – clinics with Mexican doctors who have offered their services free. We can't hope to cover the need but we can help with some of the problems. There is a sense of community and many women who previously had no political involvement but were forced to flee because of the government policy of attacking civilians, have become very committed to the cause.

Francisca, CUMS representative, Mexico City, June 1983

In Costa Rica, weekend workshops for women refugees were established by AMES and proved so successful that in June 1983 a training centre was opened. The great majority of refugees are legally recognized and receive basic assistance from the United Nations through the Costa Rican government. The training centre is organized jointly by a group of Costa Rican women and AMES and receives financial assistance from a Swedish women's organization, the 'Swallows'. The aim of the centre is to train women in a variety of technical skills including some which, for Central America, mark a break with the usual concept of women's work: electricity, accountancy, the manufacture of kilns and clothes-washing machines. The Costa Rican National Training Institute has also offered Salvadorean women places on a course to learn tractor-driving.

While there are only just under 200 women registered at the centre, AMES hopes it will soon expand. With an estimated refugee population of 10,000 in Costa Rica, the vast majority women and children, there is an obvious need. AMES has been undertaking home visits to promote the centre and make contact with women who have become very remote from events in El Salvador.

In Nicaragua, the approximately 20,000 refugees have been assisted through a special government programme. They have all been given legal status in the country and enjoy the same social welfare benefits as Nicaraguans. Their basic needs receive attention and they are assured accommodation, medical attention and food. Three production co-operatives have been established for Salvadorean families although, sadly, women have not been included in the work rotas. About a quarter of the refugees are living in camps and the government plans to incorporate them into co-operatives as soon as possible. At Leon camp, where some 1,000 refugees live, sewing, weaving and carpentry workshops have been established, together with a small school which also offers literacy classes for adults.

The women's organizations in Nicaragua and *ANDES 21 de junio*, the teachers' association, have arranged weekly visits to the camps to talk to the women about the political situation in El Salvador and to help them organize collectively:

ANDES 21 de junio, the teachers' union has produced a booklet as part of their literacy campaign which is called 'Women in Co-operatives', with a discussion theme for both sexes on shared domestic responsibilities.

Women in Co-operatives

Let's transform reality:

** When forming co-operatives, let's take into account that a woman is also a producer.
** Let's learn to value and carry out the work that, up until now women have been doing.
** In the new society, which we are creating, men and women are fighting to be true *compañeros*, both responsible for domestic work, so that both may fulfil responsibilities in society.

The women in the camps are beginning to work in small income-generating projects, mostly handicraft production, dividing whatever they earn between every family. The training of health monitors and literacy teachers is also very important. For many women, it's the first time they have been given a responsibility of this kind. In this way, women are beginning to take charge of their lives. On the domestic front, our big drive – and to date our big failure – has been to get the few men who live in the camps into the communal kitchens and to share in other tasks, like washing their own clothes, for example. They'll help with the heavy work, carrying wood or bags of grain, but not the cooking or washing up. There was an interesting experience at Leon which the women did not really take up afterwards. During the floods last year, the camp had to be evacuated. The women and children were sent into the town until the floods subsided and the men were left to guard the camp. Nothing for it, but they had to cook for themselves. But once the women returned, the men weren't prepared to lift a finger to help. We've taken the issue up on a number of occasions and some of the younger men agree that perhaps things should change, but the older ones are adamant about what they regard as women's work.
Irene, Public Relations Commission, CUMS, Nicaragua, May 1983

Mental Health

Many women refugees suffer from acute mental health problems, most particularly crippling depressions and anxieties. Some women and children have become exceptionally withdrawn or almost catatonic. The reasons are all too obvious: children in the camps, when asked to draw a picture about their lives at home, almost invariably produce

113

The woman in the wheelchair had been tortured by the army. Several of her children and grandchildren have been killed. Her daughter stands behind her. Refuge for displaced persons. San Salvador

Mike Goldwater

Mike Goldwater

Women prays in the cathedral, Sal Salvador on Palm Sunday.

scenes including helicopters bombing their farms or bodies dripping with blood flowing down the local stream.

Few refugees are fortunate enough to receive professional help with mental health problems. In Mexico City, the Latin American Health Workers' Group has specialized in helping Central American refugees and offers individual and group therapy. They suggest that one of the principle problems confronting refugees is the feeling of guilt at having left relatives in danger or for being alive when so many have died.

Case Notes of a Salvadorean Refugee from the Latin American Health Workers' Group in Mexico

Maria is very perturbed in our first interview. Her complaints are essentially physical: my head aches, my mouth, my stomach, I can't sleep, etc. She has no words to express her tension and sadness but can only identify the pain through her body.

Slowly, feelings of distress and claustrophobia (underground, bus), start to emerge, which frighten her and make her feel as if she is losing her memory. Only after several sessions is it possible for her to link these symptoms with her experiences in prison.

In our first session, Maria had mentioned that she had been in prison, but made little of it. 'I was only there five days, they only beat me, I wasn't there long.' At this stage, I don't ask any questions but let her talk about her health, her worries about her children and anxiety about her relatives in El Salvador.

Only two sessions later, the subject of prison comes up again. I ask her to tell me more. She tells me the story, showing no emotion. She was held for five days but she only knows it was five days because the people who found her, dumped by the roadside, unconscious, covered in blood and badly beaten, told her the date. I help her to see that if she was left in the road, it can be deduced that it was thought she was dead. She accepts that this is true and says she hadn't thought of it like that. From this moment on, she is able to talk more about those days and particularly about other experiences related to death and dead people.

She was responsible for identifying corpses found in different places as she was a human rights worker. She would memorize the person's clothing and characteristics and would then write the reports to be sent to the United Nations and other agencies.

She talks about how at first the proximity of these corpses frightened her and what an effort it was to look closely and have to touch them.

It is possible to link these three experiences and to show her the relation between these dead bodies which frighten her, her own experience of 'being dead' and dumped on the road and her present suffering. Her physical pain shows that she is still alive and negates her experience of death.

From this case history, we can perhaps deduce that for many refugees and political exiles, who have experienced imprisonment, these frequent psychosomatic complaints are, apart from being an expression of distress, a new way of 'feeling alive'. This allows them to negate, forget or minimize all these traumatic experiences related to facing death in such violent and sinister conditions.

In this case, we can also read between the lines to find a feeling of guilt at being alive when so many have died. An 'aching body' is a way of saying 'I'm alive – but only just.'
June 1983

In Nicaragua, an alternative approach to mental health problems among refugees is being put into action. A pilot project has been started in the refugee camp at Leon, where the resident psychiatric social worker has decided to set up discussion groups on mental health and is encouraging the community to use its own resources:

The problem of depressions and anxieties is much too widespread for individual attention, but we also believe that through community self-help, difficulties can be overcome in a much more satisfactory manner. Many refugees come to see the medical doctor or the nurse not because they are really physically ill but because of emotional tensions – headaches and unidentified pains. So we have decided to prepare a number of simple pamphlets on mental health and related problems. The first one is about 'nerves', which is the term the refugees use for depression. Others will be on the problems of exile, alcoholism and emotional crisis. We are training a group of mental health monitors from the refugee community who will be able to lead discussion groups using the pamphlets and also spot special cases of need for referral to us. This training will also be very useful in the future during the reconstruction period, as community mental health workers are going to be essential.
Psychiatric social worker, Leon refugee camp, Nicaragua, May 1983

This type of community work with refugees is in many ways similar to the organization of the controlled zones and is regarded as the basis for a future development model after the triumph of the FDR–FMLN.

Notes

1. *Amnesty International Report, 1983* (London, 1983), pp. 139–40.

Part 4: The New World

14 Women in the Controlled Zones

There are some 250,000 Salvadoreans now living in regions which the FMLN forces have controlled for a considerable period of time, in some cases for up to three years. Initially they were areas of strong support for the radical campesino organizations and the FMLN forces, but they have now expanded to cover over one-quarter of national territory. While the exigencies of the war obviously create special demands, the FMLN have placed great emphasis on the involvement of the local population in the military, political and social organizations of their controlled zones. The FMLN regard the participation of the local population as a crucial element in the ideological war against the government, at the same time providing vital practical support now and experience for the future during the reconstruction period after their victory.

> Right from the beginning, we argued that the revolutionary process in El Salvador could only be carried out through a popular war in which the incorporation of the civil population is essential ... When we take over a village or settlement and the enemy forces are ousted ... we begin the work of consciousness raising about the situation of the country together with the work of organizing the local population. The people of the village or settlement continue to carry out their normal activities but now form part of a new popular government which is set up and begins to function.[1]

The largest controlled zones are found in the north of Chalatenango Department on the border with Honduras where some 45,000 Salvadoreans live, about one-quarter of the total population of the department, and in Morazán on the north-eastern border with some 40,000 Salvadoreans. There are smaller pockets of control in the departments of San Vicente, Usulután and Cuscatlán. The latter is the department bordering on the metropolitan area of San Salvador and the FMLN forces dominate an area of approximately 350 square km around the Guazapa Volcano, only some 30 km from the capital. Some 35,000 Salvadoreans are living in this controlled zone.

The population of the controlled zones consists of the FMLN combatants, who live in military camps, and the civil population of the area, both locals and those who have chosen to join in the work. Many campesino refugees prefer to move to a controlled zone rather than cross the frontier into Honduras. The defence of the zone is organized jointly by the FMLN forces and the popular militias. The political and social organization is in the hands of the Popular Power Councils, elected through the Popular Assemblies:

> Elections are carried out at grass-roots assemblies, directed by members of the local Popular Militias . . . Anyone at the assembly can nominate a person or persons whom they consider most appropriate to take on certain responsibilities.[2]

A council covers an area with a population ranging from 200 to 600 people and is elected for a six-month or one-year period of office. While there is no absolute norm, the usual composition of the council is a General Secretary, with five or six members responsible for organization, health, education and culture, production and distribution and legal affairs. It meets every week to discuss community problems and arrange the distribution of tasks. While membership in any organization is voluntary, obedience to the 'laws' of the Popular Power Council is obligatory. The different local councils co-ordinate their activities with varying regularity and a number of national meetings have taken place. In Chalatenango, a permanent Local Government Executive was elected in May 1983, which administers affairs for the whole zone. At that time, the government forces maintained only six military garrisons in the department. This new local government has plans to draw up a law of commerce to stabilize prices and avoid speculation, and a law of public order. It has also begun the work of building a new civil register for births, deaths and marriages.

The government's scorched earth policies aim to isolate the FMLN and eliminate both their sources of supplies and their popular support. The result is quite the opposite. Campesinos flee into the controlled areas, find they are welcomed, incorporated into different areas of production and that both health and education needs are given at least minimal attention.

Co-operative Production

One of the major tasks of the councils is to stimulate production through co-operatives, both in agriculture and local industries. Products are shared between the civil population and the combatants. The FMLN command argue that co-operative production is vital, so as to develop a more self-sufficient economy within the zones and so that after the victory, the national economy will have a working base on which to build. Most important, the campesino population is experiencing a radical change in their working conditions based on a new sense of egalitarianism.

Land worked on a co-operative basis in the controlled zones has either been expropriated from the large landowners who fled when the FMLN forces took over or has been donated by middle or small range campesino families. The FMLN motto is: 'land is collective property, it belongs to everyone and is for everyone'; and they are undertaking the first steps towards a genuine agrarian reform. In accordance with the FDR–FMLN programme, there have been no wholesale expropriations and private land is respected:

> Initially agricultural production was organized by the Supplies Teams of the military camp, which either directly controlled land and organized production teams or gave seeds and fertilizers to campesino families to work their own plots. The campesinos kept enough for their families' needs over the year and handed the rest of the harvest in to the Supplies Team. Occasionally land was redistributed. For example, when a family had more land than they could work by themselves and another family had nothing. This of course would cause frictions and everyone from the municipality would be called to an assembly to explain why the distribution was necessary and just. I was working in the middle of the coffee region and so the Supplies Team was also in charge of the coffee plantations. Normally it was the women who did the harvesting, working some four hours a day. In exchange, they would be given cheese or other foods. There were some campesina women who wouldn't accept anything but worked in the fields as their form of helping the revolutionary forces. Now the co-operatives have been well established and agricultural production has advanced considerably.
> Ana, Mexico City, June 1983

The production co-operatives are made up of men, women and children. Members of the military forces must also fulfil a quota of work in the fields. Most basic crops are cultivated, but conditions are difficult. Land is often not very fertile in the controlled zones and there is always the problem of military incursions or air raids. Government forces have been known to poison water sources used for drinking and irrigation. However, in some of the better established areas, self-sufficiency in one or two crops has been reached: maize in Guazapa, beans in Usulután, sugar and rice in Morazán. In Chalatenango, Popular Power stores have been opened, selling rice, maize and sugar, some with a 'popular restaurant' attached. There is a working distribution network between the zones and supplies are exchanged.

There is a basic shortage of livestock, such as cows, chickens and pigs, mainly because fleeing landowners have deliberately killed their animals. Consequently, meat and milk are not available in sufficient quantities and it is rationed on an equitable basis. For example, in Guazapa, children receive five glasses of milk a week – but even such small quantities represent a significant advance for the majority of campesino families, accustomed to a diet restricted to tortillas and beans. In some areas, fishing co-operatives or honey production have been organized and all the zones have established a variety of small artisanal industries run as co-operatives. Shoes, clothing, leather goods, candles and kitchen utensils are all produced.

Health and Education

The FMLN has established hospitals with small professional medical teams. The smaller clinics are under the control of the Popular Power Councils and are run by health promoters who place particular importance on basic health education and preventive medicine. Reflecting a general attitude to democracy and participation at a grassroots level, primary health services are provided by people with no formal training but who possess a basic grounding in good health practices. They argue that First World medicine has created a powerful elite whose services are costly and do not reflect the priorities of Third World countries. They are trying to undermine dependency on professional care and, through education for self-help, allow people to take more control of their own health. As the most common cause of death in El Salvador is preventable gastric disorders, health education and technical improvements to the water systems can be astoundingly effective in improving general levels of health..

Similar attitudes pervade adult literacy and primary education programmes. Education should be relevant to the needs of the community and knowledge should be shared:

> In the camp where Radio Venceremos operates, there are 15 women and some don't know how to read and write. So what happened is that the literate women arranged their time so that every day they now have an hour set by to sit down with one of the illiterates and that's how the literacy campaign is operating at the moment. It is regarded as an individual revolutionary task for each of us to teach someone else who doesn't know how to read and write.
> Campesina woman from Morazán[3]

A new culture is also developing in the controlled zones which tries to incorporate traditional campesina culture into the themes of the liberation struggle. Popular theatre and music groups reinterpret the theatre-dance, the *sones* and *boleros* still found in the rural areas of El Salvador. These date back to the Spanish colonial period but much has been lost because of the impact of commercialized Western culture.

The 'Torogoces', a music group named after a bird renowned for the beauty of its song, perform in the Morazán controlled zone. They are a group of campesinos who are all engaged in other work. Some are combatants and others work in agriculture. They describe their music as giving culture back to the people, allowing them to find a new identity and respect for their collective cultural history.[4]

Women in the Controlled Zones

The organization of women in the controlled zones varies considerably depending on the region: either one of the women's organizations has taken on the task or there may be a women's committee of the Popular Power Council. In Chalatenango, for example, AMES has been given full membership on the local government executive in recognition of the importance of their work in mobilizing women.

The women's organizations have been instrumental in promoting women's rights, particularly the need to train women to assume responsibilities outside the domestic sphere. They are running various workshops and co-operatives which were initially started through the financial support of women's groups in Europe and elsewhere.

> Women are doing what they can in the controlled zones – this means anything from making tortillas and looking after the kids to political and military work. The important thing to emphasize is that women are given the opportunity to participate in all areas of work and that there exists a definite attempt to organize and train women for tasks outside the domestic sphere. One finds many women who are in charge of supplies, or working in the munition workshops, in tailoring, shoe-making, pottery or local manufactures, such as hammocks and so on. They are also working in the fishing co-operatives, where the women clean and salt the fish while the men do the actual fishing. In the La Laguna area in Chalatenango the fishing processing co-operative is officially run by AMES.
>
> The work women are carrying out is by no means easy. In supplies, for example you often have to undertake almost military type operations. I witnessed a group of 150 women who planned and carried out an ambush of the enemy to requisition bread and flour and the only arms they were carrying consisted of sticks and cords. To be a nurse also requires a lot of mental equanimity and physical strength. You have to perform operations while listening to gunshots and rescue the wounded, collecting their weapons while carrying a rifle and a medicine chest.
> Claribel, Nicaragua, May 1983

While most campesina women are still generally involved in different forms of service work, some have taken on elected political posts in the Popular Power Councils, including that of General Secretary. Many middle-class women students have gone to the FMLN camps from the cities to work as doctors, nurses or in information and educational services. Ana worked for a year in the *Frente Paracentral 'Anastasio Aquino'*, one of the controlled zones in the centre of the country, with the team in charge of information and political education. There were seven women and five men in the team. A member of the BPR, she had just entered the state university, the UES, to study journalism when she was asked whether she would like to take up the work:

> I decided to commit myself to the revolution and in January 1981, went to the Frente Paracentral, which at that time covered parts of the Departments of

Cabañas, San Vicente and La Paz. The total civilian population in my sub-zone numbered some 7,000 and there were nine FMLN camps in the area, the Chinchontepec Volcano. Our job was to write the military communiqués, the leaflets explaining our political programme and what we were fighting for when we moved into a new municipality, prepare tapes for the occasions we occupied the local radio stations in San Vicente and Zacatecoluca, monitor the international and national radio stations we could reach, and produce the mural newspapers for all the sub-zones of the region. Every week we used to produce 30 mural newspapers, containing national and international news, small biographies of combatants who had been killed and information to commemorate important dates in the popular movements of our country.

Life was pretty tough. We lived on a small farm which had been partly burnt down, some 1½ km from the main military camp. We slept in hammocks, on mats and newspapers and there was no water or electricity. We could only use candles at night if we were working, because they were in very short supply. The food was scant: weeks when the only thing available was tortillas and salt. Then there would be a requisition, like the time when the Supplies Team got hold of 100,000 eggs and that was great. Sometimes we would go into the hills and find wild fruits and we began to grow a few things, like cucumbers and tomatoes, but it was generally hard going.

We would get up at 5.30 a.m. every morning and do 45 minutes of exercises. Then we would prepare breakfast, which would mean fetching the water and collecting wood for the fire, which the men usually did, while two women would be in charge of making the tortillas. Then about 8.30 a.m. we would begin the work of the day, eating again at mid-day and at 6 p.m. We were asleep by 8 p.m. but would have to take it in turn to keep guard, not just against the enemy but also the cows!

When I was there, in May 1981, the government troops organized a big invasion of the area, involving some 3,000 soldiers. They used helicopters, airplanes and mortars. But the area had been well prepared for an attack. We had to withdraw into the hills, taking the civilian population with us. Each campesino had been given instructions to always have ready 20 extra tortillas in case we had to leave at a moment's notice, but even so, it was very hard.

We had to walk for about a week, sleeping during the day and continuing at night. There was strict discipline and we weren't allowed to make any noise in case we were heard. The women not only carried all the possessions they didn't want to risk losing in large baskets on their heads but also had to control their children and often had to sling them over their backs as they were too weak to walk themselves. There was virtually nothing to eat and two children died of starvation.

It was hard to see how everyone was suffering. We spent 20 days out of the zone before it was safe to return. But there was no choice – if we had stayed, or if only the civilian population had remained behind, the army would not have hesitated to massacre everyone. As it was, when we eventually returned, we found everything had been destroyed – houses, crops, animals. It was like starting from scratch all over again.

Ana, Mexico City, June 1983

Women Combatants

Women's participation as combatants is less marked than in other work, although there are renowned women in important military positions, such as Comandante Ana Guadalupe Martínez, a highly skilled urban combatant who has now become a member of the FDR Political-Diplomatic Commission and the late Comandante Ana Maria, who was second-in-command of the FPL. Many of the combat fronts have two or three women comandantes at one time in the six-person military command, such as the *Frente Oriental 'Francisco Sánchez'* which presently has three women comandantes. In the FMLN camps in Chalatenango about 30% of the combatants are women.

The proportion of women combatants has risen considerably over the last three years. Initially, as many men have recounted, there was a great deal of prejudice about women's military capacities:

> I knew men who simply refused, or at least, found it very awkward, to salute a woman military leader who was their superior in the ranks. It just went against the grain. So the male comandantes would make a special point of saluting women comandantes in front of their troops as an example for them. But even now, a woman has to achieve much more than a man in order to gain respect or 'promotion'. She has to be triply brave, triply astute on missions to win the recognition a man would receive.
> Claribel, Managua, May 1983

> The first time I came up against a woman comandante . . . I realized just what a macho I was at heart. I felt it was wrong. Wrong to trust a woman with the responsibility of leading a hundred soldiers on a mission. I was convinced she would muck the whole thing up!
> Pedro, Mexico City, June 1983

Women have preferred to act as collaborators, as messengers or guards or offering their houses as meeting places, all of which subject them to considerable risk. They have also provided essential support in urban military operations:

> We use older women in the urban organizations. These women go out with their children and in their bags or baskets, instead of carrying nappies or extra clothing for their children, they have the bombs or weapons which we will use a few blocks further on.[5]

But as the repression has increased, more women have directly joined the combat forces. Elena described her feelings on returning to the little town of her birth, San José de las Flores, in Chalatenango after three years' absence. She had left to become a combatant with the FPL and is responsible for a health brigade. She returned with the FPL to take over the town which has now been incorporated into the Chalatenango controlled zone:

> I was born and lived here, ran along these streets. With my parents and

127

brothers, I took part in demonstrations to protest against the repression and to support the economic and social demands of the campesinos from this region.

Now I've returned. I found that my house had been used as a barracks, everything we possessed has been destroyed. There's nothing in the house except a few empty boxes of arms and munitions sent to our government by the North American regime.

In 1978, my parents moved to San Salvador to carry out tasks for our organization. The National Guard murdered them. Two of my brothers have also been killed. The rest of the family decided to join the guerrilla forces. Thinking of our dead parents and brothers makes us determined to continue to fight against this repressive government.[6]

Over the last two years, there has been a determined drive to incorporate more women into the military ranks by offering them special training programmes. In Chalatenango, a training school was opened for women interested in joining the military command. After a six-month course, the women trainees were asked to conduct an army ambush as proof of their military capabilities and once they had passed this test, were then sent to different battalions.

The all-women Sylvia Battalion was formed in December 1981 and has fought in the Guazapa Volcano region. Ileana, who leads the battalion, is a young woman, only 20 years of age. She joined the *Fuerzas Armadas de Liberación* (FAL) at the age of 17 after two years as an active member of the *Juventud Comunista*. The battalion became famous for a skilful defence of the Cerro Mala Cara carried out in February 1982, when the combined forces of the US-trained army battalions, the 'Ramon Belloso' and the 'Atlacátl' were forced into retreat:

The enemy becomes particularly demoralized when they realize that it is a unit of women behind the line of fire making them retreat. This was made very evident when someone in the Belloso Battalion shouted across to the Atlacátl Battalion, who were on our left flank: 'Attack! It's only women firing at us' and the Atlacátl replied: 'Why don't you? It's not sweets they're firing on us!'[7]

Ileana felt that women had won a new respect after this military operation, not only from their own organization but throughout the FMLN. There are now other women's squadrons, and women are also sometimes trained separately in the civil militias. Consulted about these arrangements, many women choose to work only with other women as it inhibits them less.

Many women combatants must make the hard decision to separate themselves from their children and compañeros. Usually there is no formally organized system of child-care and most women leave their children with relatives. Some camps have recently opened nurseries for women who wish to keep their children with them.

Although pregnant women are obviously forced 'out of action' for some time, birth control is an individual decision:

Everyone has to make up their own mind and define their own position with respect to the revolution and maternity. If a woman combatant decides to have a child, then her organization helps her resolve the practical problems.[8]

There are many difficulties in getting supplies through to the zones and priority is given to medicines, not to contraceptives. Campesina combatants are generally opposed to using contraceptives for religious reasons and while women from urban areas may wish to adopt some form of birth control, it is not always available:

In some zones, there is no family planning available, nor much sexual education to tell the truth. Women use limes as a contraceptive but they are not very effective and with frequent use the vagina can be seriously damaged by so much acid.
Claribel, Managua, May 1983

In some zones, abortion facilities are made available to women combatants:

When a women is politically involved, the decision to have or not have a child becomes a political decision as well and not just a question of personal wishes. Women who have become pregnant and don't want to have a child – if it's been a mistake – have been able to have abortions.
Campesina woman from Morazán[9]

While the way in which sexual relations are conducted obviously varies considerably from individual to individual and from zone to zone, generally speaking, there is an attempt to maintain a fairly strict control in the military camps, although this does not apply for the civilian population, nor should it be regarded as an indication of future attitudes. In Chalatenango, for example, the FMLN forces maintain that by preference, sexual relations should not occur outside of a matrimony (understood in a broad sense and not implying either a civil or religious ceremony). First, it is felt that too much 'sleeping around' may provoke jealousies and rivalries damaging to military morale. Secondly, with so many adolescents within the combat forces and given the communal living arrangements, there exists a sense of responsibility for their education and a feeling that they should not be lead into promiscuity.

Personal Relations and Sexuality in the FMLN Camps in Chalatenango

Claribel is a film-maker who has made a film about women's lives in the controlled zones, entitled *Road to Freedom*. She was interviewed in May 1983 in Managua while editing the film. She emphasizes that these are her personal observations from

---

Chalatenango and are not necessarily true for all the camps:

How is marriage and the couple understood in the FMLN camps in Chalatenango?

The formation of a revolutionary matrimony is taken very seriously. The two people involved inform their respective comandantes and ask permission to enter what is known as the first stage of a relationship, where sexual relations are prohibited but the couple can spend time together. The couple must then explain to their comandantes why they think their matrimony would work. The second stage is reached when they are officially recognized as a couple. The natural birth control method is explained to them and they are told that, given the war, it would be much better if they do not have children because a pregnancy is a big problem in the camps.

How are separations dealt with?

A separation also has to be discussed with the comandantes and difficulties in the relationship explored. A couple doesn't have to stay together come what may, but normally an attempt is made to discover the problem. For example, there was one couple who asked for a separation but talking with their comandantes, they came to the conclusion that the real problem was they hardly ever saw each other. So the comandante arranged for them to spend more time together and everything worked out well.

Are relations outside a recognized couple frowned upon?

When sexual relations occur outside a recognized couple, normally the man is demoted from whatever position he holds. It's quite easy to know what's going on because of the communal life-style of the camps. I would say that those kinds of problems are found among the middle classes, more influenced by the morals of the United States but that among the revolutionary campesinos, the men are more faithful. They assume a revolutionary morale more readily.

What happens in the case of rape?

Rape is a crime which is very severely punished. The man involved has to go before a tribunal composed of the military units of the man and woman involved, which decides on the punishment. It's a form of popular tribunal. Normally the man is imprisoned in a hole in the ground for 15 days, with nothing more than his head out of the ground. They do this so he will think about his crime and also to show the whole community that the revolution considers rape as a criminal act and not just something that happens as part of daily life, which is still the attitude of many people. I don't know of any case where the man has committed rape for a second time. His *compañeros* speak to him, explain why such behaviour is not acceptable. We aren't in a position to give psychiatric treatment and neither is it possible to tell the culprit to leave the camp. But we have to show that we are not like the army of the government, which as a matter of routine, always rapes women when carrying out a military operation. Their military commanders not only tolerate such behaviour but actively promote it. We have a totally different attitude towards women.

Notes

1. José Ventura, *El Poder Popular en El Salvador* (Mex-Sur Editorial, 1983), p. 63.

2. Ibid., p. 67.

3. 'Interviews with Women', *Radio Venceremos Transcripts*, mimeo (Mexico, D.F., January 1982).

4. Manuel Sorto, 'Las Torogoces de Morazán', in *Palo de Fuego, Revista Cultural Centroamericana* (Mexico, D.F., Oct.–Dec. 1983).

5. 'Interviews with Women'.

6. Transcript from the film *El Camino de la Libertad*, Instituto Cinematográfico de El Salvador Revolucionario, 1983.

7. Norma De Herrera, *El Papel de la Mujer en la Revolución Salvadoreñá* (Editorial Claves Latinoamericanas, Mexico, D.F., September 1983), p. 28.

8. *Uno Más Uno*, Mexico City, 12 December 1981.

9. 'Interviews with Women'.

15 Changing Lives

Women's vision of their future in a new society is closely related to their own experiences and education and whether they have been in touch with the women's movement outside of El Salvador. Some suggest that a new society will bring an end to the repression, the constant fear, the torture, the deaths and disappearances. It will mean they can return home, either leaving the refugee camps in San Salvador or ending their enforced exile abroad, to start to rebuild their homes in the knowledge that the army will not descend on them again. It simply means peace.

Others, who have experienced life in the controlled zones or are members of one of the mass organizations, express wider expectations. In the country, they hope they will work in co-operatives, share the work and the produce, find a new sense of community in their lives. They expect immediate gains in terms of agrarian reform, medical services, greater opportunities to attend school, a literacy campaign. They believe it will mean that for the first time in El Salvador's history, there will be genuine political freedom.

There are few women who talk about changes in terms of 'women's rights', although many are highly critical of machismo, the double exploitation of women, the imposition of family planning. Some, through their contact with the various women's organizations, are aware of these problems and believe that change is already taking place in many very positive ways.

We asked men and women what they understood by the oppression of women, what changes the new society would bring for them and what they hoped to contribute to that new society. Salvadorean women cannot begin the practical experiment by which they hope to change their lives – now largely a theoretical debate – until the country's right to self-determination is respected.

Women participate in the national liberation struggle and have never considered they should be struggling to liberate themselves from men. They are fighting against all types of repression and injustice found in our country. They have their own demands but they are an integral part of the liberation struggle, which, right from the start, has stood for equal rights for men and

women. Women's participation in the movement has developed a great awareness about women's particular needs, in terms of nurseries, the socialization of domestic work, etc. These needs are already understood and it will not be the function of a women's organization in a new society to fight for such rights. In the future, a women's organization will take part in the collective work of national reconstruction.
Ana Lilia, human rights' worker, May 1983

The new family is a new form of understanding. Fathers don't have the sole authority in the home and mothers don't see their role as servants to men. In the new family, both men and women will make the decisions, they will be equal partners. My husband doesn't feel ashamed to be seen sweeping with a broom or carrying the child and in El Salvador, those are new attitudes.
Betty, market woman from ASUTRAMES, February 1983

I am convinced that the subordination of women is at the root of the distribution of power within any society. Our aim is to break down patriarchal and hierarchical power within the family. There is still not much awareness that the personal is also political and we want to change this situation.

After the triumph, we will have to concentrate on educational work so that women are at last in a position to express demands. We wish to draw up a family code to protect women's rights in the home and to ensure that the family becomes a more socialized structure. My personal wish is to work with women in education and training programmes and information resources.
Maria Novoa, AMES representative, July 1983

We want to change the way children are brought up. We are not going to use violence, we are not going to tell girls they can't go out and play in the streets, that they have to stay at home. We want children to learn without fear. They should not learn different roles depending on their sex, nor should learning be based on punishments but on respect for their understanding and potentialities. In the family, we hope to create relations based on a real equality, in which women are productive, the children independent and husbands respectful.
Marta, social worker, July 1983

One of the most important changes I expect to see after the revolution is in the situation of children. I hope that gradually we will stop seeing them begging on the streets without any prospects for their future. Our society has produced children who are not only miserably poor economically but who are also spiritually empty. In contrast, it is extraordinarily encouraging to think that after the revolution, they will be guaranteed a basic diet, access to medical services, education and recreation and that they will be living in a creative and open society.
Rosa, journalist, June 1983

I never heard the word 'feminist' in El Salvador. I have always been in contact with women trade unionists, or Christian communities, or organizations such as ANDES *21 de junio* but they weren't specifically women's organizations. I believe that the new man and the new woman are totally related to the new society, which we all know is socialism. As Christians, we want this society to be more humanitarian, more based on criticism and self-criticism, more about sharing and equality. In many ways, this has already taken place in the Christian communities.

A woman should be just as committed as a man to the construction of justice and love. Women's role will be to take part in this work of construction after the revolution. Maternity will also be important but that doesn't mean giving the country 20 sons. In the new society, we believe that a husband or children will not act as a limitation on women.
Sister Guadalupe, nun, June 1983

Right from the beginning, we have actively encouraged women's incorporation. Because there are so many women in the Popular Leagues, LP-28, we are sometimes jokingly called the 'Feminine Leagues'. I don't think that after the triumph, we are going to experience a drop in women's involvement. Attitudes have really changed and it's not just a question of superficial behaviour. We see these changes as essential to the revolution. Beyond a change of government, the revolution has much more ambitious aims: the creation of the new human being. In 1977, when I joined the organization, it was more than apparent that the other women did not have the remotest idea about women's liberation, felt that doing the cooking for men was their political contribution, etc. To think how much we have changed surprises me.
Claudia, student of psychiatry, June 1983

The fact that women have decided to participate in the difficult but just struggle of El Salvador has meant that they have developed politically and ideologically and that there have been many changes in men's attitudes. After the triumph, I believe these changes will become more apparent. In the future, women's rights will be respected and men will become more critical and more conscious of the way they relate to women.
Pedro, journalist, June 1983

The Catholic religion has marginalized women, in part, one might say, since it was decided that God was male. In the nuclear family, women are either seen as 'mother' or 'lover', the root cause of the unhealthy machismo of Salvadorean men. Now women participating in the liberation struggle are finding new roles. Obviously we are not going to cure the blight of centuries in a few years. But after the triumph, I don't have the slightest doubt that women will ensure that their true rights are respected. Women will no longer accept that they are relegated to the kitchen or are treated as machines for the production of children.
Ricardo, painter and writer, June 1983

I believe feminism helps women overcome cultural obstacles stemming from their family relations. The social struggle is also part of the feminist struggle – at least in our country's context – because the restructuring of the social system will help overcome these obstacles, although the pace of change will not necessarily be in a strict mathematical equation.

A new society means, above all, giving a new value to individuals. For the first time, Salvadorean women will know the meaning of self-respect, whereas before, not even human life was respected. Women are the historical

'have-nots' and as a consequence, they take over what they consider to be their only 'possessions' – their children. So, in turn, children become dependent on their 'all-protective mothers', immature all their lives and unable to assume responsibilities. Many become dependent on alcohol as a result. The cycle is repetitive: abandoned children of irresponsible fathers, women forced by circumstances to be strong and to take sole responsibility for their children. But all this is gradually changing because the civil war is creating new relations between men and women and that implies a transformation in men *as well*.
Tina, writer, June 1983

The main thing is the national liberation struggle. Feminist demands are out for the moment. What is happening is that women have shown their competence in practice and this has helped to change machista attitudes. But beyond the incorporation of women in the revolutionary organizations and the fight against machismo, we will have to wait until we can implement structural changes in the economic and social system.
Julia, FDR representative, November 1982

The revolution must give women their place but it is a long process which won't happen immediately. A lot depends on women because we must show men what we are capable of. Nothing is going to be handed to us on a plate; on the contrary, everything must be fought for and that's why women's organizations are necessary.
Liliam, AMPES representative, July 1982

In Central America, we have no other way of achieving women's emancipation except through revolutionary changes in the economic, political and social system.
    Salvadorean women have two main demands: the right to the self-determination of our country and the other, an end to our oppression as women. For that reason, a women's organization linked to the revolutionary process is very important.
    Our demands are those which the present government has always denied us – the right to organize, wide participation in the political life of the country, access to education, together with our social rights, good health, decent housing, and voluntary maternity.
    Women have a great task to accomplish – something along the lines of what one of our revolutionary leaders once termed 'the revolution within the revolution'.
Miriam, CUMS representative, May 1983

Feminism is a movement which emphasizes the values and rights of women. In the new society after the triumph, men will play a very important part in this movement. We are not going to treat men as the enemy but both sexes will have to fight against the same ideology.
Gloria, ANDES *21 de junio* representative, December 1982

Feminist liberation is bourgeois and talks about such things as the legalization of abortion. I would say that feminism is imperialist. Women participate, not as feminists, but as revolutionaries to free ourselves from

135

exploitation. Machismo is the result of the capitalist system and men treat women as objects only good for the bed. All this has to be overcome with comprehension both at home and within the community.
Magdalena, FSR trade union representative, May 1982

After the triumph, women will no longer be over-protected, exploited and raped.
Amanda, factory worker, February 1982

After the revolution, I hope to return home, work in the fields, take care of my animals, the chickens and pigs and grow my vegetables again. I would also be prepared to take up some responsibility in the popular government. It will be a less oppressed life, more tranquil, although perhaps at home there will only be me because my husband and my two sons have been murdered by the army and the others have gone to fight. I think women will receive more help with childbirth, we will have a clinic near by, someone who will take an interest in our health and the education of our children. We will work collectively in co-operatives so as to be able to help each other.
Susana, campesina, July 1983

16 Postscript: Marianella García-Villas

Marianella, a lawyer, journalist and founding member of the CDHES in 1978, first brought to the attention of the world, perhaps more than anyone, the massive scale of human rights violations in her country. Initially a member of the Christian Democratic Party and elected the youngest Congressional deputy in 1974 at the age of 26, Marianella resigned from the party in September 1979 on the grounds that the Christian Democrats were not serious about the denunciation and investigation of human rights violations.

From then on, she devoted her life to human rights. Her work was extremely painful and very dangerous – the examination of corpses, daily visits to the body dumps around San Salvador, the taking of testimonies from relatives of the disappeared. She knew she could be killed at any moment. Marianella was detained and tortured by the security forces on two occasions in 1978 and her name appeared on many death squad lists. Her parents' home was raided and destroyed and her family was forced into exile.

The offices of the CDHES were twice raided and bombed and as a consequence, in 1981, Marianella decided to move the main offices of the CDHES to Mexico City. She had to live with the memory of the death of many of her fellow-workers. Maria Magdalena Henríquez and Ramon Valladares Perez were murdered by security forces in October 1980. In December of the same year, three other members of the CDHES, Carlos Vides, Francisco Cortez and Norberto Huezo Martínez were captured and remain disappeared. In August 1982, América Fernanda Perdomo was detained by the Treasury Police and also remains disappeared. In February 1983, yet another member of the CDHES, Dr José Roberto Martelli, was detained and disappeared.

Marianella was assassinated on 14 March 1983, at the age of 34, in circumstances which will never be clarified. She had returned to El Salvador in January to collect evidence on the use of chemical weapons by the Salvadorean army, in order to present a report to the United Nations. At the time she was supposedly killed, she was in a combat zone, monitoring a Salvadorean air force raid. The first statement issued by COPREFA, the armed forces press office, declared that she had been killed in combat and claimed she was a guerrilla combatant who operated under the name of Comandante Lucia. COPREFA later retracted this statement, recognized she was a human rights worker and decided she had been caught in the cross-fire when she died.

A delegation of the International Federation of the Rights of Man (FIDH) of which Marianella had been Vice-President, was immediately sent to El Salvador to investigate the case. They reported that all the evidence would indicate that Marianella was assassinated by the armed forces after having been tortured and raped:

> Marianella was not injured in the cross-fire. A young woman who was with her hid when she heard the first shots and witnessed what happened. Marianella was taken alive by a group of soldiers and put into a helicopter. It would have taken 15 minutes to reach San Salvador and Marianella was probably transferred for interrogation to the Military School. An official inquiry indicates that her body arrived at the Military Hospital at 16:20 the same day and came from the Military School. One must fear that Marianella was in their hands for 10 or 12 hours ...

> I've never seen such a bullet-ridden corpse. However, both the judges' report and the autopsy do not prove that her death was caused by those bullets. There are signs that she had been tortured: severe cuts, her legs broken, her right arm dislocated ... I believe she was tortured to death. She was probably raped first as she had a horrible wound in the abdomen, undoubtedly caused by a grenade, as if to make an examination impossible.[1]

Marianella lived under enormous pressure and sometimes imposed upon herself an almost overwhelming work schedule – two or three nights without sleep were not uncommon. Despite the tensions of the human rights office, she was always remarkably good-humoured and adored the few social moments she allowed herself. She had a well-earned international reputation and received many awards for her human rights work. Above all, Marianella will be remembered as a very brave and very determined woman.

Note

1. Statement given by the President of the Spanish League for the Rights of Man and Vice-President of the International Federation of the Rights of Man, Antonio García Barraja, as published in *Primer Semestre del Año de 1983: Los Derechos Humanos en El Salvador* (Comisión de los Derechos Humanos de El Salvador, September 1983, Mexico City), pp. 25–7.

Appendixes

Appendix 1

The Federation of Salvadorean Women: Statement of Principles and Objectives

The conference of Salvadorean women's organizations held in July 1984 agreed to set up a Constitutive Committee with a view to forming the future national women's organizations, the Federation of Salvadorean Women. The following Statement of Principles and Objectives was adopted at the conference:

Principles
1. The incorporation of women is an inseparable part of the struggle of our people, which is fundamentally the fight against imperialism and oligarchic rule.
2. Without the true liberation of our people, the marginalized and oppressed situation of women will not be changed. Our struggle is for the liberation of our people.
3. We are struggling for peace with justice.
4. Our Federation believes in international solidarity.
5. Our Federation will establish contacts with other associations of democratic and progressive women, who also struggle for the right to life, for peace in the world and against the arms race, imperialism, apartheid, zionism and all types of oppression, domination and exploitation.

General Objectives
1. To fight for national sovereignty and the right of our people to self-determination.
2. To inform people about the situation of Salvadorean women and children and their fight to claim their rights.
3. To contribute to the creation of a just and more democratic society and for the construction of a provisional government of broad participation.

4. To fight against imperialist intervention in El Salvador and Central America and to unmask the pro-imperialist and oligarchic nature of the present regime in El Salvador.
5. To call upon all the relevant national and international organizations to respect the rights of refugees and displaced persons.

Specific Objectives

1. To fight for the demands of women in all areas: political, economic, legal and cultural.
2. To increase the participation of women workers and campesinas and women from other social sectors and to mobilize them in the democratic, anti-imperialist and anti-oligarchic struggle.
3. To denounce the lack of respect for the life and human rights of women in our country.
4. To denounce the repression against women, children and the population in general, perpetrated by the Salvadorean regime.
5. To create a united front of Salvadorean women so as to improve solidarity and contacts at an international level with other women's organizations, whether humanitarian, legal, etc.
6. To undertake campaigns, projects and other activities so as to promote solidarity with our people, specifically directed at international women's groups and other relevant organizations.
7. To co-ordinate work with the Salvadorean mass organizations on specific issues.
8. To increase the solidarity of other peoples with our cause and motivate them to campaign more actively against North American intervention in our country and in Central America.
9. To develop broad solidarity with women and peoples in struggle.
10. To create contacts with the international women's movement and all democratic and progressive organizations who are fighting for the equal participation of women in society.
11. To ensure that the Salvadorean people, in particular women, are well informed and recognize the Federation and that a network of information is created.
12. To ensure that the relevant international organizations take the necessary measures to assist orphans, displaced families and refugees of our country.
13. To promote specific activities in our country, such as the commemoration of important national and international dates, campaigns, etc.

APPENDIX 2

Publications by Salvadorean Women's Organizations

Asociación de Mujeres de El Salvador

1. *Colección Luz Dílian Arévalo*
a) 'Como nacemos y que hacemos'
b) 'Posición de AMES frente a la paz, la distensión y el desarme'
c) 'Desde los frentes de guerra'
d) 'Desarrollo de la participación política de la mujer salvadoreña en el proceso de la liberación nacional'

All published Mexico City, 1983.

2. *Boletín Internacional*, Trimestral año 1 – Sept. 1981.

3. 'Participación de la mujer latinoamericana en las organizaciones sociales y políticas – reflexiones de las mujeres salvadoreñas'.
Paper presented at the first Latin American Seminar on Research on Women, San José, Costa Rica (8–14 November 1981).

4. 'La mujer y la niñez salvadoreña, víctimas de la represión militar'.
San Salvador, May 1982, Mimeo.

APPENDIX 3

Addresses of Salvadorean Women's Organizations

Asociación de Mujeres de El Salvador (AMES)

Costa Rica
Apartado Postal 7522
San José, Costa Rica

France
c/o Femmes Solidarité El Salvador
68 Rue de Babylone
75007, Paris

Mexico
Apartado Postal 20-134
México 20, D.F.

Nicaragua
Apartado Postal 1000
Telcor Central
Managua

United States
P.O. Box 40311
San Francisco
California 94140

P.O. Box 1308
Brooklyn, New York
11234

P.O. Box 41146
Chicago, Illinois
60641

Asociación de Mujeres Progresistas de El Salvador (AMPES)

Mexico
Apartado Postal 22-072
Tlalpan
México 22, D.F.

Asociación de Mujeres Salvadoreñas (ASMUSA)

Nicaragua
AP 228
Las Piedrecitas
Managua

Comité Unitario de Mujeres Salvadoreñas (CUMS)

Mexico
Apartado Postal 21-310
Colonia Roma
Delegación Cuauhtémoc
Mexico, D.F.

Appendix 4

El Salvador Since the Election of Duarte

by Mandy Macdonald

Since the main text of this book was written, an elected civilian government has taken office in El Salvador. Office, but not power. Power in El Salvador still rests with those who have held it for the last half-century: the army, the big landowners, and the right-wing politicians who represent their interests. Behind these figures looms that of the United States. Ronald Reagan has also been elected, for a second term; and the American right now feels less reticent about backing the Central American right. Ironically, the election of a civilian government in El Salvador seems to have unlocked the floodgates of US aid which, by giving the Salvadorean army the military edge over the armed opposition, in effect puts off indefinitely any peaceful settlement to the conflict.

For the FMLN forces will not give in easily. They are preparing for a long war – even longer than it has been to date. But while it is being waged, its principal casualty will continue to be – as it has been for five years – the civilian population. At very conservative estimates, there are now well over 50,000 dead; half a million refugees; another half million homeless and destitute in their own country. The civilian government has done nothing about that – except to allow the army to bomb civilian targets, massacre villagers, and drive civilians at gunpoint out of the FMLN-controlled zones. It has done nothing about the plight of landless rural workers – except to snuff out the last flickerings of an agrarian reform that might have offered them the security of a little plot of land. It has done nothing about the urban poor – except to neutralize public sector strikes by promising wage rises which it cannot pay (or else to repress them with violence), and to transfer to the consumer the burdens of a war-wounded economy. And it has done nothing about the paramilitary death squads – except to fire one or two of the most glaringly implicated military officers and pack a few others off to sinecures abroad.

The United States Administration wants a military defeat for the Salvadorean revolution; and the Duarte government – if we are to judge by its actions and not its rhetoric – wants that too. This resumé of events in 1984 and the first half of 1985 reflects on the government's failure –

without either political freedom to act or political will – to do anything in the interests of the vast majority of its citizens.

US Aid to El Salvador (millions of dollars)

	FY82	FY83	FY84	FY85	(request)
Military Assistance	82.0	81.3	196.5	128.2	
Economic Support Funds	115.0	140.0	210.5	195.0	
Economic Assistance	67.2	91.1	120.65	131.1	

Central America Report 20 (Jan/Feb 85) p. 6

The Return to Civilian Government

The 1984 elections were held against a background of continuing civil war, economic crisis and rising labour discontent. As in 1982, only the centre-to-right band of the political spectrum took part. The official British observers to the elections, Dr David Browning and Sir James Swaffield, wrote:

> We do not agree with the view that representatives of the FDR–FMLN would have been able to participate freely and securely in the election campaign ... had these representatives campaigned openly they would have run a very high risk of being assassinated.[1]

Though the US poured millions of dollars into a supposedly fraud-proof computerized system of voter registration (which broke down on the day), bureaucratic bungling of stupendous proportions probably prevented more people from voting in the first round (25 March) than did the FMLN's mass confiscations of the identity cards people needed in order to vote. After a second round, a Christian Democrat government headed by José Napoleón Duarte took office on 1 June 1984.

But these were presidential, not general, elections, and although Duarte had gained 53% of the vote, he was to wait a year before the Legislative Assembly and municipal elections of March 1985 gave him even a parliamentary majority. In the meantime, without a clear majority in the Assembly, under pressure from both the powerful landowning private sector and the resurgent labour movement, and straitjacketed by the armed forces and the US Administration, Duarte was throughout 1984 unable to achieve anything except diplomatic recognition, continued (and vastly increased) US military and economic aid, and the surprise offer, in October, of talks with the FDR–FMLN.

Of the parties which took part in the elections, only the Christian

Democrats (PDC) had even a rudimentary platform to offer the nation. Together with the other centrist party, the small Acción Democrática (AD), the PDC committed itself to an eight-point national policy which included 'defence of democratic institutionality'; 'pacification' – arriving at a state which would 'allow political space to all tendencies, making a common meeting ground of ideas possible again'; the defence of human rights, curbing the actions of 'groups which violate human rights'; the 'efficacious application of justice'; economic recovery 'with the combined efforts of the different sectors'; 'social development' for all sectors.[2] In practice, this implied taking steps to lessen the more visible human rights abuses (clamping down on the death squads, investigation of the murder of Archbishop Romero and of US citizens in El Salvador such as the four churchwomen killed in December 1980) without which Congress would not release further military aid funds. It meant calming the nerves of the private sector, whose natural sympathies lay firmly with the right, while implementing the 'Social Pact' Duarte had signed with the large Popular Democratic Union (UPD), a centrist confederation of trade unions and peasant organizations, in order to secure its votes. It even apparently meant the possibility of dialogue with the armed opposition – but not negotiation: 'I don't believe in incorporating guerrillas into a democracy', said Duarte. And it meant a fanfare of rallying calls to the army, the business sector, the unions, and the right-wing parties, to pull all together for the good of the country.

In reality, however, the Duarte government was the government the United States wanted. The CIA had pumped a million dollars into the PDC's election campaign.[3] It was not surprising that Duarte's first act as president-elect was to set off for Washington, from whence he returned with a tasty prize: $62m in aid, unfrozen by Congress by the mere fact of elections having been held. 'Reagan has to support the right', said FDR president Guillermo Ungo in an interview with the Mexican newspaper *El Día Internacional* in February, 'but ... in an election year, he has to disguise it. And the best disguise is a moderate candidate and a moderate party, with a fairly progressive vocabulary.' [4] More importantly, it was US *military* policy that was served by the election of this apparently moderate, reformist candidate. The Reagan Administration was not – is still not – interested in a peaceful settlement in El Salvador. If it were, why was military aid to El Salvador multiplied practically 30-fold between FY 1980 ($6.7m) and 1984 ($196.6m)?[5] But Congress, and particularly the liberal Democrats, had become increasingly uneasy at the idea of pouring aid (much of which was being drained away by corruption in any case) into a military government with one of the worst human rights records in Latin America, even in the name of containing the Soviet–Cuban–Nicaraguan threat. So a Christian Democrat government, led by a candidate who was very much a known quantity for Washington, was promoted, behind whose facade the US, and the

Salvadorean oligarchy and armed forces, have continued ever since to pursue the military defeat of the FDR–FMLN.

No Room to Move

Holding only 24 out of the 60 seats in the Legislative Assembly (the result of the 1982 election), the PDC government was handicapped from the start. Moreover, though most of the 37 Cabinet ministers were Christian Democrats, and none of them *arenistas*, all the key posts in financial administration and the judiciary went to right-wingers such as the National Conciliation Party's presidential candidate Francisco Guerrero as president of the Supreme Court and PAISA's Dr Rafael Flores as attorney general. Through this institutional control, the right proceeded to block practically every move of Duarte's which did not tally with their interests. An early victory for them came when the Assembly voted to terminate the four-year-old agrarian reform programme, revoking Article 207 of the law which governed Phase III of the reform, entitled 'Land to the Tiller' and providing for large-scale distribution of lands to small peasant farmers.

The right also had effective control over the national budget. In a real slap in the face to the executive, the Assembly slashed the 1985 draft budget from ¢2,433m ($973m) to ¢2,033m ($813m), making particularly severe cuts in the presidency and administrative areas where the PDC was strong, while actually increasing the salaries of top right-wing civil servants and magistrates. The agriculture ministry's agricultural research and extension programme was axed completely from ¢23m to a 'symbolic' sum of ten *colones* – just enough to ensure its nominal existence.[6] The National University, which had been under military occupation since June 1980, was returned to its governing body on 21 May 1984; an estimated ¢80m ($38m) was necessary to rebuild and re-equip it. None of that money has ever been made available.[7]

The government was perhaps most visibly hamstrung by the right in its attempts to carry out even limited human rights reforms. On election Duarte took a series of initiatives designed to show that he was taking seriously the US Congress's admonitions about improving El Salvador's human rights record. He set up a 20-man presidential commission, reponsible to himself, to investigate human rights violations by the security forces. Its 1985 budget was cut, along with those of three other presidential commissions. Col. Nicolás Carranza, whose name had frequently been linked to the death squads, was dismissed as head of the much-feared Treasury Police (Policía de Hacienda) and that force's special intelligence unit was dismantled. But Gen. Eugenio Vides Casanova, who had also been linked with the squads, and who had even been implicated in covering up the murders of Archbishop Romero and the four US churchwomen,[8] is still Duarte's minister of defence. A number of other officers connected with political assassinations and repressive activities, such as Capt. Eduardo Avila and Lt. Roberto López Sibrián (responsible for ordering the shooting of US labour advisers Michael Hammer and Mark Pearlman and agrarian reform institute head Rodolfo Viera in January 1980), were disciplined but not convicted. 'Duarte might be mad', said a high-ranking officer at the time of the election, 'but he's not stupid. He knows that if he tries to get rid of the security forces we'll overthrow him.'[9]

Clean-up Operations?

'The Salvadoreans have cleaned up their act', said a US State Department official in July 1985; 'a lot of the garbage in the middle and upper ranks are gone.'[10]

Statistics on political killings, arrests and disappearances might seem to support this view: comparing figures quoted by the Christian Legal Aid of El Salvador (*Socorro Jurídico*, one of the three NGOs which records cases of human rights violations from within the country), there were 2,506 arbitrary executions or assassinations of non-combatants in 1984 as against 5,670 in 1983; 668 arbitrary detentions (1,265 in 1983); 116 forced disappearances (326 in 1983). Socorro Jurídico's estimates are on the conservative side, but they do reflect a drop in individual cases of human rights violations reported to the institution. However, as they point out, their figures reflect only the cases reported to their San Salvador office: very often, 'instead of turning to the humanitarian institutions located in San Salvador, the inhabitants of certain rural areas affected by both serious violations of human rights and clashes between the government armed forces and the insurgent forces generally flee the country or refrain from denouncing the events for well-founded fear of reprisals ... The non-governmental institutions for the protection of human rights had major difficulties in conducting direct, *in situ* investigations of the serious collective violations of human rights ... mainly committed against the civilian population in rural areas ...'[11]

The period of office of the Duarte government has seen an alarming rise in the number of aerial bombings of the civilian population carried out by the armed forces, mostly in the countryside. Recently these are being followed up by infantry sweeps which produce massacres. According to the Salvadorean opposition news agency Salpress, these reached an average of 40 a month in the first half of 1985 (total 242).[12] Bombings and massacres have only quite recently begun to receive coverage in the international press; but testimonies collected in June and July 1984 by a British human rights worker from survivors who ended up in the church-run refuges in San Salvador show that the practice is widespread.[13] Operations of this kind, particularly against villages in the guerrilla-controlled zones, have been justified by army sources as a way of flushing out guerrillas from their civilian support, or simply of frightening that support away – but a more cynical view came from Salvadorean officers who complained that local people 'got in the way of military operations' and that anyway 'they were all guerrilla collaborators'.[14] Certainly some of the air weaponry provided by US military aid seems designed to do more damage to civilians than to smaller, more mobile groups of guerrilla fighters. Examples are the AC-47 plane, capable of firing 1,500 rounds a minute, and the Hughes 500 helicopter gunship, adapted to prolonged low-altitude pursuit of slow-moving targets and capable of 6,000 rpm.[15] Both these are modified versions of aircraft used by US forces in Vietnam.

At the same time, individual human rights violations continue to occur. The periods leading up to both the 1984 and 1985 elections have been particularly violent. Archbishop Rivera y Damas attributed eight deaths in a week just before the 1985 polls to right-wing death squads; FMLN forces were also responsible for the deaths of some right-wing politicians. But while President Duarte has constantly assured the people, the church, and the US Congress that something is going to be done about the death squads, there is little evidence of it, apart from a few cosmetic sackings of embarrassing figures such as López Sibrián. And the death squads have not disappeared. New ones have sprung up recently, and old ones, such as the Secret Anticommunist Army (ESA) are still active, even if they keep a lower profile. A group calling itself the 'Traditional Catholic Movement' sent death threats to the archbishop and his auxiliary bishop Gregorio Rosa Chávez early this year. That month CDHES gave details of 24 people arrested or disappeared by security forces or paramilitary groups.[16]

Nonetheless, the return to civilian government, with its attendant 'peace-and-justice' rhetoric, did give space in 1984 to the few human rights organizations which can work at all in El Salvador. The Committee of Mothers of the Disappeared, Murdered and Political Prisoners 'Oscar Arnulfo Romero' (known as the 'Comadres') took to the streets, holding weekly protest marches of up to 200 women through the capital, demanding the return of their missing friends and relatives. Their work reached a high point on 5 November in a large peace march through the capital, in which 3,000 people participated – the first time for years such an event had been possible. The march itself was not suppressed or attacked by the authorities, but in the days following it a number of the participants were picked up by police and security agents. The Comadres were awarded a prize for their human rights work by the Robert Kennedy Foundation – but only one of the five-woman delegation which set off for the United States to receive the award was granted an entry visa. The others were turned down on the grounds of 'connections with subversive activities'.

Another example of the political opening available in 1984 to human rights campaigners was a well-attended conference on human rights held in San Salvador at the end of November. It was organized by the Comadres, among other groups. But the horizon is darkening in 1985: on 12 June the building which houses the offices of both CDHES and the Comadres was raided and cameras, tapes, documents, and money removed. The Comadres were sure security forces were responsible. On 10 July, three days after a vigil held by 75 women from the two committees of mothers and relatives of the disappeared, María Esther Grande, one of the Comadres, was arrested at her home by security agents.

Perhaps President Duarte should be left with the last word on human rights. In 1981, when he was acting president at the head of the civilian-military junta, the rector and staff of the Catholic University in San Salvador protested strongly about the shooting of a student by security forces on the university campus. Duarte's attitude towards human rights may be measured by his reply: that national security takes priority over human rights.

Who Pays the Price of War?

> The social and economic costs of the war and its apparatus are incompatible with any effort ... [either] ... to start a real recovery of the country's productive structure ... [or] ... to make concessions simultaneously to business and labour while transferring the costs of the war to them both.[17]

Five years of civil war have devastated an economy that was dependent and debt-ridden before the war began. By the end of 1984 the war effort was eating up over 40% of the national budget, costing a million dollars a day. These soaring costs were mirrored in a staggering fiscal deficit ($240m), a huge foreign debt ($164.8m) [18] and an acute dollar shortage despite massive injections of aid. Unemployment was around 30–40%, inflation stood at 42%, and real incomes per capita had dropped by 35% since 1980. Production of El Salvador's major export crops has fallen steadily since 1979/80.[19] Cotton and coffee lands have been abandoned as their owners left the country, taking their capital with them. For those landowners who stayed, there has been little incentive to invest, even were there sufficient funds available, since the country's agroexport sector has come increasingly into the FMLN's firing line. In December 1984, guerrilla sabotage in the eastern coffee-growing zones alone was reported to have totalled ¢10.8m ($4.32m).[20]

This faltering economy is crucially dependent on foreign aid, and perhaps Duarte's only achievement in the economic field has been his success in obtaining not only vastly increased amounts of US aid but also aid agreements with other countries. (The EEC recently announced that it is to double its economic aid to Central America, including El

Salvador, over the next five years.) A slight (1.5%) upturn in GDP for 1984 was, in fact, due almost entirely to the high level of US aid.

But much of the US aid is military aid and goes directly into the war. In June 1984 the new president told *Playboy* magazine:

> ... the aid is given under such conditions that its use is really decided by the Americans and not by us ... how many planes or helicopters we buy, ... how many trucks we need, ... how many pairs of boots ... It is decided by the one who gives the money. And all of the money is spent over there. We never even see a penny of it, because everything arrives here already paid for.[21]

And the economic aid has come hedged about with insistence on the part of AID and the IMF that the government 'create' money by devaluation of the *colón* or equivalent measures, which inevitably result in further price rises and inflation. The agroexporters are also firmly in agreement with devaluatory measures. Mostly these have consisted of the transfer of more and more items to the parallel market. In September 1984, AID made disbursement of $50m in economic aid conditional upon the transfer of a large number of products onto the parallel market, plus increases in public service charges and guaranteed prices for the coffee and cotton crops – a move for which the private growers' associations had long been clamouring. The most recent transfer of goods to the parallel market was in June 1985. The process affects not only 'inessential' or luxury goods but has been extended to major export crops and imported industrial inputs.

The agribusiness oligarchy are traditional holders of economic power in El Salvador. They form the backbone of the political right wing, especially ARENA. They have the support of the army, and the US, as the September AID conditions made explicit. They also bring in the export earnings so desperately needed not only to attempt any recovery of El Salvador's productive apparatus but also to carry on the war. Politically, Duarte's need to placate the private sector, if he is to placate the right, has always taken priority. Economically, every strategy the PDC government has so far come up with has placed the private sector firmly at the centre of 'economic reactivation',[22] together with small business and the public sector. But politically the private sector, represented by the National Association for Private Enterprise (ANEP) and the associations of cattle, coffee and cotton producers, is well aware that it holds the winning cards and has lost no opportunity to wring large concessions from the government.

The repeal of Phase III of the agrarian reform is an example. Another is the substantial concessions granted to cotton-growers, who declared a production stoppage on 15 May 1984, demanding better credit facilities and a guaranteed price of ¢110 ($44) per *quintal* (cwt) of their crop.[23] The outgoing provisional president, Alvaro Magaña, acceded to the cotton-growers' demands after only a week; in the meantime thousands of public employees were on strike for wage rises and over non-payment of wages. Throughout 1984, private coffee-growers were demanding first the denationalization, then the abolition, of the state coffee board INCAFE, calling it 'an unconstitutional restraint upon trade'. By the end of the year ARENA had brought in a bill declaring INCAFE unconstitutional, which was referred to a select committee of the right-dominated Assembly.

However, the subsidies the government has made to business and landowning interests have been in almost every case made at the expense of the PDC's own actual or potential social base. Even after an August meeting between Dr Fidel Chávez Mena, minister of planning and author of the Christian Democrats' 'national strategy for economic reactivation', and representatives of agrarian unions and co-operative federations, the government still seemed 'more favourably inclined to listen to the demands of big capital . . . than to the proposals of the small business sector',[24] with predictable 'weakening of the PDC's social base, which consists to a large extent of small businessmen'. And by September the UPD was complaining bitterly that the PDC had reneged on their joint social pact, dropping the agrarian reform, dragging its heels on a political solution to the war, and failing to implement wage settlements to the public sector which had been promised in April.[25]

In fact, Duarte's approach to the labour movement has been to make some minimal concessions while keeping up a steady crescendo of anti-union rhetoric. The urban labour movement, particularly the public sector unions, was not slow to take advantage of the political space opened to it by the election process itself and the installation of a professedly reformist government. Strikes proliferated in the 1984 runup period, till in late March 25,000 public sector workers were reported to be striking. A 10% wage rise was agreed to in April,[26] but the incoming government was in no position to implement it. Months later, public sector unions were still striking for implementation of the 10% rise – 6,000 were out in early July –and in an attempt to head off fresh strikes and avert a political crisis, the treasury ministry presented the Legislative Assembly with a draft proposal for a general salary rise of ¢130 for all public employees, probably to be financed by measures which would in practice result in an increase in the cost of public services or indirect taxation to the consumer.

Some 1,400 postal service workers did receive a ¢150-a-month wage rise after a six-week strike for very moderate demands including uniforms and two pairs of shoes a year for postmen. A number of other Salvadorean unions staged work stoppages in support of them and some countries refused to handle post to and from El Salvador.[27] As a result of their action, too, nine trade unionists arrested in a January raid on the FSR congress were released in July. Later, in August, the 17 STECEL (power workers' union) prisoners, who had been in prison without trial since August 1980, were – somewhat suddenly – also released.

But as the essentially incompatible claims of labour and capital put the government increasingly under strain, Duarte came down ever more heavily on the side of 'his former business enemies rather than [that of] the workers who had supported the Duarte programme';[28] and as the year wore on the reformist tone of the honeymoon period gave way to accusations from the government that strikes were 'politically motivated, designed to destabilize the economy',[29] or that the United Trade Union Movement (MUSYGES) were Communists who were driving the country into bankruptcy.[30]

1985 has seen a new clampdown on the unions, despite the consolidation of the PDC government at the Legislative Assembly elections. Amid rumours that guerrillas, chased out of the highland zones, were flocking to the cities to join the urban labour movement, reports have appeared that the Treasury Police are receiving training in urban counterinsurgency. In May, invoking 1980 labour legislation (passed under Duarte's previous administration) outlawing public sector strikes and subjecting the workforce to martial law in times of trouble, security forces militarized water and sewage works whose personnel were among the 50,000 currently on strike. Forty-nine members of the waterworkers' union were arrested.

On 2 June the president again accused the unions of trying to destabilize the government, at the instigation of the FMLN. That same day, over 500 police and National Guardsmen stormed five hospitals and 20 clinics in the capital, crushing a month-long strike and sit-in by 4,500 health workers demanding a wage rise and payment of back pay. Union leaders were arrested and a patient died in the raid. Public outcry at this violent strikebreaking was such that the government subsequently awarded the health workers a pay rise of ¢150 a month and corrupt administrators were sacked. But the outlook for the labour movement is increasingly sombre, as repressive forces seem to be readying themselves again for conflict in the cities.

Testimony from the hospital raids of 2 June

On 2 June I was in the Social Security hospital when we heard, it must have been, two helicopters landing on the terrace of the building. It was about three in the morning. A bit later we started to hear shots, and I got out of bed to look out the window.

In no time the hospital was in chaos. I went out to the service area by the labour ward, where patients wait before the birth of their child. As I entered the ward I came face to face with a masked man in a dark camouflage uniform (= black fatigues?) and with a gas mask. Later I found out he was a member of the Treasury Police. I put my hands up, and he shouted at me to get down on the floor, face down. All the while you could hear people running about the hospital, and there were lots of shots. It was chaos.

When they made me lie down on the floor, they did the same with the doctors and nurses. They tied everyone's hands together. They kept us like that an hour and a half, as though we were criminals, tied up with twine. I've still got the marks of it on my arms. While we were tied up and lying face down like that they shouted insults and threats at us; they said that if we moved they'd kill us. They were very tense, the assailants. They shouted, they asked questions; but we didn't understand what they wanted to know; what they were after, and that only made it worse. If you didn't answer them, they hit you, and if you lifted your head from the floor, trying to see who it was asking you the question, then they hit you too.

The patients in that ward weren't made to lie on the floor because they had equipment attached to them, to monitor how the baby was; but, although they cried out in distress, the assailants wouldn't let the doctors attend to them. Later I discovered that in all the other wards they treated everyone the same way. They had them all down on the floor, doctors, nurses and patients, even women who'd just given birth. No respect for anyone.

When we got up, after about an hour and a half on the floor, an announcement was coming over the loudspeaker system that there was an emergency case. One of the patients was crying and vomiting, with a serious infection. Later I found out that at the beginning they hadn't allowed any of the doctors to see to her, and when they did allow it, it was too late. A woman doctor went to her and managed to start her heart again, but because of the delay, the damage to her brain was irreparable, and she died around eight o'clock that morning.

Around six a.m. a man arrived who I later found out was Major Rubio. He ordered them to untie us. By then we all had bruises on our wrists and very sore arms. The major apologized, he said he was only obeying orders, because they thought there might have been armed men in the area.

When they released us, the doctors went to do the rounds of the patients. Everything was in disorder and panic. That was really when we first pieced together what had happened. As well as the men who'd come in the helicopters, who said they were from the Treasury Police, there was also another security corps, who came in through the emergency ward. So it was a joint operation. But when they encountered each other the two groups got confused and they ended up shooting at each other. Where this was happening there happened to be a nurse there; she got so panic stricken that she started to run, and they shot at her too, but luckily it was dark and she wasn't hit. The emergency ward was all spattered with blood.

We also found out how it ended. There were two trade unionists in the auditorium; when they saw the security men ill-treating patients, doctors and nurses they identified themselves as trade unionists and gave themselves up so that the raiders would leave us alone. They were both taken away.

> I came away out of the hospital still shaking with fear. It was all like some incredible nightmare. I don't think they found any arms, but the arms they were carrying terrified everyone. I never would have thought such things could happen in a hospital.
>
> *Carta a les Iglesias 93* (1-15.6.85)

As 1983 ended, the FMLN forces were in a strong position. FMLN-controlled zones covered some 20% of national territory (about 4,000 sq km) in Chalatenango, Morazán, parts of Santa Ana, Cabañas, La Unión and San Miguel, and the Guazapa volcano north of the capital. On 29 December 1983 guerrillas took the important El Paraíso garrison in Chalatenango department, and three days later, on New Years' Day, they blew up the Cuscatlán bridge, which connects eastern El Salvador with the rest of the country. Both these actions showed that the FMLN were able to take the military initiative and put the government forces under considerable strain. Army casualties at the year's end were high, about 20%, and the army leadership was looking for 'new tactics and a new methodology' as the election campaign got under way.

Bridging the Gap

In January 1984 the FDR/FMLN called for the setting up of a broad-based provisional government (GAP), to include representatives of manual workers, peasants, teachers, white-collar workers, professionals, the universities, political parties, business interests, the opposition coalition itself, and a new army, purged of repressive elements.

This government's basic aims would be to recover national sovereignty, eliminate human rights abuses, end the war, meet the urgent needs of the population, and prepare for general elections.

Measures would include:

● and end to the State of Siege
● freedom for political prisoners
● the abolition of security forces (other than the army), death squads and the ARENA party
● a purge of the army, and the incorporation into it of FMLN combatants
● an investigation of human rights abuses
● an emergency reconstruction plan
● a nationwide literacy campaign.

Central America Report 19 (Nov./Dec. 84), p. 2

Also at this time, the FDR–FMLN made new and serious attempts at starting a process of negotiation with the government, publishing in early February a proposal for talks and a provisional 'Government of Broad Participation' (GAP) based on their earlier programme.[31] This was rejected outright by all parties. In fact, far from acting on its pre-election pledges to seek a peaceful solution to the war, the new government stalled, while the military proceeded to use the massive injections of US aid released by the holding of elections to boost its air power, particularly stepping up aerial bombing raids helped by US-supplied OV-1 Mohawk spotter planes. While the guerrillas responded to these tactics by breaking up into smaller units and moving out into new areas, the main brunt of the bombing was borne – and is still being borne – by civilians. By mid-1984, bombing of civilian targets had reached unprecedented levels.[32]   Not surprisingly, the guerrilla-controlled zones came under heavy attack.

The guerrilla forces, however, were moving out from their bases in the north and east of the country into the strategically important central zone and – later in the year – the west, hitherto relatively untouched by combat. They began also to concentrate their attacks on small military outposts and on roads, bridges and the electricity system. This sabotage campaign, striking at the government's increasingly fragile economic base, characterized FMLN actions throughout 1984 and into 1985; but there were some large actions, such as the seizing of the country's biggest hydroelectric plant at Cerrón Grande (28 June 1984), when over 70 soldiers were killed or wounded, hostages were taken, and extensive material damage was caused.

As harvest time approached for El Salvador's main export crops, sabotage actions were extended to these too. In July 1984 Radio Venceremos had warned cotton-growers that the FMLN would hinder the planting of the crop and exhorted them to plant food crops instead. Later in the season they concentrated on burning the ripened crop and on sabotaging lorries carrying cotton, coffee and sugar to the ports.[33] The labour-intensive growing and harvesting of coffee was not attacked.

The FMLN proved that it could still carry out large co-ordinated actions by a big attack on Suchitoto on 9 November; but by the end of the year the tide was beginning to turn. US military aid to El Salvador was $196m for the financial year ending October 1984, the highest it had ever been. The army's helicopter fleet grew from 24 to 49 between September and December,[34] vastly increasing army mobility. *This Week* commented, 'by January the airfleet will have the capability of flying a battalion of airborne infantry to a conflict point within minutes.' This meant that the guerrilla forces could no longer rely on their classic tactic of keeping the army pinned down in a number of small actions in several places at once, thus stretching its resources to the limit. Now the army, too, could be everywhere at once.

Popular church mass in a refugee camp   *Paolo Bosio*

Refugee camp — Honduras   *Paolo Bosio*

Mike Goldwater

Entrance to a controlled zone

Operation Torola IV, at the end of October 1984, marked the first time helicopter-borne troops were used on a large scale, when 2,000 troops were flown into Morazán, close to guerrilla positions, with fighter-bomber support. As usual, the main victims of this tactic were the civilian population (over 600 refugees fled across the Honduran border in four days between 14 and 18 October); but an important military casualty was Lt. Col Domingo Monterrosa, commander of the San Miguel-based 3rd infantry brigade, who died with a number of other officers when their helicopter exploded on 23 October. Monterrosa was regarded as the Salvadorean army's most able strategist and his loss was a severe blow to the army.

There were other changes in the army high command, too. One of the most significant was the posting of Lt. Col Sigifredo Ochoa Pérez to head the 4th infantry battalion, based at the key El Paraíso barracks in Chalatenango. Ochoa is a chief exponent of US military thinking around El Salvador, particularly its counterinsurgency aspects. He is also, together with air force head Juan Rafael Bustillo and chief of staff Adolfo Onecífero Blandón, a close crony of Roberto D'Aubuisson's from military college days. Blandón, Bustillo and Ochoa were by late 1984 the ascendant faction within the high command, and the promotion of all three at the end of the year heralded a new and more sophisticated strategy against the guerrillas – heavier bombing, the use of military hardware like the AC-47 and the Hughes 500, a more developed counter-insurgency strategy, and a more intransigent attitude to negotiation.

War with Peace

In this context it is perhaps surprising that any progress towards a negotiated settlement should have been possible at all. But throughout 1984 moves in this direction were being made both inside and outside El Salvador. The proposal put forward by the FDR–FMLN in Mexico on 9 February 1984 was by no means their first step towards negotiations. They had been periodically offering dialogue since December 1980,[35] and on four occasions in 1983 FDR representatives had met US special envoy Richard Stone and the Salvadorean government peace commission in Bogotá and San José, as well as making several diplomatic initiatives aimed at obtaining international recognition of a state of belligerency in El Salvador and consequent application of the Geneva conventions. For the first half of 1984 there was an impasse: the Frentes reiterated their openness to dialogue, while standing by the terms of the GAP, which included a purge of the army's repressive forces and the incorporation into the army of FMLN combatants; Duarte insisted that, while dialogue was theoretically possible, there could be no negotiation until the rebels disarmed unilaterally – a step which they not unnaturally refused to take. Then, in a sudden volte-face dramatically revealed at the United Nations General Assembly on 8 October, Duarte proposed a meeting with the FMLN leaders at La Palma in Chalatenango the very next week, on 15 October.

Swamped with media attention, attended by 50,000 Salvadoreans from all points of the political compass, and held in an emotional atmosphere almost of jubilation, the La Palma meeting was probably more significant for having happened at all than for anything that resulted from it. A joint investigative commission was set up, to be chaired by Archbishop Rivera y Damas, who had acted as mediator at the meeting; efforts would be made to 'humanize' the war; and a second meeting date was set for late November. FDR president Guillermo Ungo called the talks an important first step which allowed everyone to 'view the future with greater optimism'.[36] Two days later, Torola IV began, and the troops went into Morazán.

The second round of talks, held at Ayagualo near San Salvador on 30 November, achieved if anything less than the first. In the weeks leading up to it, various sectors of the right began backing off from dialogue, perhaps encouraged by the re-election in November of President Reagan in the United States. According to ANEP, the only ones to benefit from the talks were 'the terrorists';[37] other right-wingers hinted that Duarte could be using conciliatory gestures to gather votes for the March 1985 elections.[38] Neither Ungo nor Duarte attended the Ayagualo meeting. Positions were stated on both sides with greater intransigence, revealing their fundamental incompatibility. The only advance was a unilateral assurance by the FMLN, made after some vacillation, of a cease fire for two short periods over the Christmas and New Year holidays. The army refused to follow suit.

'Now we have a two-track policy', US ambassador Thomas Pickering remarked after La Palma, 'war with peace'. Certainly US policy throughout seems to have been to pay lip-service to peace initiatives while continuing massively to finance the Salvadorean government's war effort. Such an attitude is revealed in the shifting fortunes of the Contadora peace process, named after the Panamanian island where four Latin American countries – Mexico, Colombia, Venezuela and Panama – met in January 1983 to set up a mediating group to work towards peace in Central America. The group has met regularly, with representatives of the five Central American countries, but there have been many setbacks. Contadora has been called 'the centrepiece of regional negotiations', a 'rare example of co-operative diplomacy in a continent traditionally dominated by the United States'.[39] But the function of a centrepiece is essentially decorative, and in over two years of discussion and drafting of peace proposals Contadora's achievements have been mainly formal. There have been several points at which, just as agreement on a peace formula is near, the US's main regional allies – El Salvador, Honduras, and Costa Rica – have raised objections. These three, plus Guatemala, even held an 'alternative' Contadora meeting in Tegucigalpa in October 1984 to draw up a modified version of the *Acta de Contadora*, the draft peace plan which Nicaragua had declared itself ready to sign at once in early September. Later, a 'sensitive' document prepared for the 30 October meeting of the US National Security Council credited US foreign policy with success in preventing a prompt signing.[40]

It is inescapably clear that US goals in Central America are the overthrow of the Sandinista government in Nicaragua and the defeat of the Salvadorean revolutionaries. These goals have been pursued as energetically in 1985 as in 1984. Few people are talking now of an FMLN victory in the short term, if at all. With their US-supplied weaponry, the armed forces are in a far stronger position than they enjoyed even a year ago. The controlled zones are under almost unbearable pressure. There is evidence that the guerrilla forces are increasingly turning to forced recruitment, hitherto largely the preserve of the army. Politically, too, the hardliners feel more confident, as the security forces clamp down on trade unions and death squad killings are on the upsurge again.

The government forces' main objective in the rural areas is now the reconquest of the FMLN-controlled zones. Two strands in army strategy came together at the beginning of 1985 in a counterinsurgency plan that was fully worked out for the first time. To the heavy bombing of the controlled zones and areas surrounding them was added a revised version of the counterinsurgency plans which had failed in 1983/4 in San Vicente and Usulután. The new plan owed its inspiration – and its motto – directly to the Guatemalan experience: *Techo, Trabajo y Tortilla* – Shelter, Work and Food. It was called 'Plan Mil', from the intention to resettle 500,000 people in 1,000 villages.

The theory behind projects like this is simple: 'Take the water away and the fish will die.' In other words, drive the civilian population – around 200,000 of them – out of the controlled zones and you will leave the guerrillas without the support and protection of their social base. This is called, in the Salvadorean army's terms, 'clearing the zones militarily'. The area is then 'militarily secured' by the formation of civil defence patrols; 'civic action' projects are implemented to 'reconstruct' and 'develop' the zone of operations (or what is left of it - Guazapa volcano has now been bombed so often that there are no trees at all left on its upper slopes); the zone is then repopulated and its inhabitants resettled.[41] The plan is accompanied by 'psy-ops' – psychological warfare, increasingly a feature of Salvadorean army strategy.[42]

In practice, it seems that Plan Mil has not been systematically put into operation. The formation of civil defence units, for instance, has been hotly debated in army circles. In some places these units have reportedly been formed, not without predictable opposition from the communities. 'We're not against the army', said the mayor of La Palma,

Chalatenango, where a civil defence unit was proposed, 'but having such a patrol could be dangerous.' And in Santa Clara, San Vicente, according to its mayor, 'the people said they'd rather leave than join the civil defence.'[43]

One element of the counterinsurgency plan that is clearly under way, however, is the clearing of the zones. In Chalatenango, one of the places where it is being put into operation, Col. Ochoa announced that clearing the zones means that 'we cannot allow any contact between the population and the rebel army. First we must separate the civilians from the guerrilla and then smash the guerrilla. The civilians will be able to return once we have secured the area.' In practice, what this meant was that all civilians were ordered to leave 12 zones which were defined by the army as 'free-fire' zones, where Ochoa would give his troops orders after a certain time to shoot anyone they encountered. Any civilian who chose (or dared) to stay, by this reasoning, must be a guerrilla and therefore a legitimate target.

A similar method has more recently begun to be used in Guazapa. This area, the closest of the FMLN-controlled zones to the capital, has been for a long time an object of particular hatred to the army, a stronghold of the 'Marxist subversives' just 25 km from the city. In late 1984, people who had fled from Guazapa told British human rights workers that it was being bombed regularly twice, sometimes three times a day, morning and evening. If they had any bombs left over after a bombing run, one refugee said, they would drop them on Guazapa on the way home, 'just out of spite'. Yet its inhabitants hung on, incredibly, tending their tiny, scattered plots, ready to drop everything at a moment's notice and run for their bomb-shelters. Now, as well as the bombing, they are being moved out bodily. Over 500 civilians were taken from the Chalatenango and Guazapa areas by the army in April. Some of them told how soldiers had literally dug them out of their underground shelters and handed them over to the International Red Cross, supposedly for their own safety.

In response to the army's new counterinsurgency programme, FMLN strategists say they are settling in for a prolonged war, concentrating on extending and stepping up sabotage, increasing actions in urban areas against selected targets,[44] and carrying out political work in the countryside and the urban labour movement aimed at showing Salvadoreans that the Duarte government is not doing its job or fulfilling its election promises. The incidents in the eastern part of the country in which guerrillas captured 14 recently elected Christian Democrat mayors and held them hostage should be seen as part of this political campaign. Guerrilla presence has also become more noticeable in and around the capital and other towns. Two spectacular actions just before election day, 31 March, were the attacks on a telecommunications point atop the San Salvador volcano (16 March) and on the National Police headquarters right in the city centre (27 March). More recently, Mariona prison, on the outskirts of the capital, was blasted on 12 July by an explosion 'apparently co-ordinated both inside and out';[45] 149 prisoners, 13 of them political detainees, escaped.

The maverick Clara Elizabeth Ramírez Front has claimed responsibility for a number of assassinations such as that of Lt Col Ricardo Cienfuegos, head of the army press office (COPREFA). But the killing of four US marines and nine others of 19 June in the expensive Zona Rosa district of San Salvador was claimed by an urban commando of the Central American Revolutionary Workers' Party (PRTC), one of the groups that make up the FMLN, and was explained by FMLN sources as a warning to US military personnel in El Salvador that the Frente now considered the Reagan administration to be its principal enemy,[46] and that US military people were no longer immune from attack.

A number of press articles early in the year[47] suggested that rebel combatants, driven out of their northern strongholds, were coming to the cities in large numbers and swelling the ranks of the labour movement. But ERP commander Joaquín Villalobos, one of a group of FMLN leaders who received a delegation of American liberals and others in Perquín, Morazán, in the second week of July, told them 'We hope to generalize the war across the whole country within a year',[48] something that would not be possible unless a majority of combatants were still active in the countryside. However, the alleged wholesale movement of guerrilla fighters into the towns provided a neat justification for renewed repression against the labour movement and new funding for security forces operating in the cities. After the PRTC attack on the marines, the US Administration quickly proposed aid grants for training and equipment to four Central American security forces, including El Salvador's.

On 31 March 1985 Salvadoreans went to the polls for the third time in four years, this time to elect members of the Legislative Assembly and local government officers in the 262 municipalities. The Christian Democrats again emerged victorious – surprisingly, since the Duarte government, with so little political room to act during 1984, could scarcely have proved effectual in the eyes of most of the electorate. The result consolidated the PDC's position, giving it at last a comfortable parliamentary majority with 33 of the 60 seats, and 200 of the town halls. The government followed up its win speedily with a reiteration of the pledges made in 1984: the search for 'peace and justice', a broad programme of health, education and social welfare provisions. There were hopes for a renewal of the peace talks – but they were dashed when an FDR–FMLN proposal for a meeting at Perquín at the end of May was turned down by the president. Meanwhile the war continues unabated. The trade unions are facing open repression, with the hospital strike being broken at gunpoint and the water and sewage service militarized. The death squads are making an unwelcome comeback: among them, a new group, the Central American Anti-communist Organization, was responsible for 48 deaths in May. The election result pleased the Reagan administration, for a more firmly based Christian Democrat government means that the passage through Congress of aid requests is smoother.

The *Washington Post* greeted the result with enthusiasm: 'Before, [Duarte] was a good bet for the United States', it said, 'and now he is a better bet.' Whether he is a better bet for the Salvadorean people, as the war approaches its sixth year, is seriously open to question. The hope for the future which sprang up in the organization of an alternative, truly democratic, society in the controlled zones is fading as the zones are bombed out of existence and their inhabitants driven out. And the Christian Democrat government has proven by its track record what was already implicit in its programme – that it is unable and unwilling to provide any real answers to the problems of the poor.

Notes

1. Quoted in *Central America Report (CAR)* 18 (September–October 1984), p. 11.

2. *Proceso* 145 (30 April–13 May 1984), p. 13. *Proceso* is a weekly news and analysis bulletin from the documentation and information centre of the Catholic Central American University (UCA) in San Salvador.

3. *International Herald Tribune (IHT)* 14 May 1984.

4. Reprinted in *Proceso* 138 (13–19 February 1984), p. 10.

5. *CAR* 23 (July–August 1985), p. 3.

6. *Inforpress Centroamericana* (Guatemala-based weekly), 10 January 1985, p. 6.

7. In recent years 29 private universities have opened in San Salvador, while between 700 and 1,000 schools have been forced to close down because of violence, lack of materials, shortage of teaching staff, etc.

8. As commander of the National Guard at the time, Vides Casanova was, according to ex-intelligence officer Roberto Santibáñez, in a position to remove all evidence of high-ranking officers' involvement in these killings, in which the hit-men were National Guardsmen. Santibáñez suggested Vides Casanova was responsible for the cover-ups in an interview broadcast in Britain under the title of 'Short Circuit' (Channel 4, 27 March 1985).

9. Quoted in *Proceso* 145, p. 12.

10. *IHT*, 26 July 1985.

11. Archbishop Oscar Romero Christian Legal Aid Service, *Human rights in El Salvador: report for the period January–December 1984* (San Salvador, February 1985), pp. 1–2. Figures from this report and their *Report for the period January–December 1983* (San Salvador, February 1984); English translation published in co-operation with World Council of Churches.

12. *Boletín Semanal Centroamericano* 188–9 (24 June–7 July 1985).

13. *We don't live in houses any more*, El Salvador Committee for Human Rights, London, 1985.

14. CDHES, communiqué, 28 June 1985.

15. NARMIC, *Invasion: a guide to the US military presence in Central America* (American Friends Service Committee, 1985), pp. 20–1.

16. CDHES, *Informe* May 1985, pp. 4–5.

17. *Proceso* 149 (25 June–8 July 1984), p. 4.

18. *Inforpress*, 11 April 1985.

19. CEPAL (Economic Commission for Latin America) figures, summarized in *El Salvador Briefing* (Central America Information Service, London), July 1985.

20. *El Diario de Hoy*, quoted in *Proceso* 169 (17 December 1984), p. 8.

21. *Playboy*, p. 73.

22. See e.g. Fidel Chávez Mena, 'El Salvador: crisis, estabilidad y proceso democrático', in *Estudios Centroamericanos* 432–3 (October–November 1984), pp. 763ff.

23. *Proceso* 146 (14–27 May 1984), pp. 4–5.

24. *Proceso* 154 (27 August 1984), p. 4.

25. *Proceso* 155 (3 September 1984), p. 3.

26. *Inforpress*, 12 April 1984.

27. *Proceso* 149, pp. 5–6.

28. *This Week* (Guatemala), 10 September 1984.

29. *Inforpress*, 5 July 1984.

30. *Inforpress*, 24 October 1984.

31. See above.

32. 42 cases from 1984 are listed in *Human rights in El Salvador* (February 1985), pp. 29–33.

33. *This Week*, 19 November 1984. *Proceso* 163 (29 October 1984) published the FMLN's table of recommended salaries and work conditions for coffee workers.

34. *This Week*, 24 September 1984.

35. *Proceso* 161 (15 October 1984), pp. 3–6.

36. *Proceso* 162 (22 October 1984), p. 3.

37. *Proceso* 167 (26 November 2984), p. 1.

38. *Proceso* 166 (19 November 1984), p. 2.

39. *CAR* 19 (November–December 1984), p. 2.

40. *El Salvador Briefing*, December 1984.

41. *Proceso* 171–2 (28 January 1985), p. 9.

42. See e.g. *Sunday Times*, 5 May 1985. *Proceso* (171–2, p. 9) reported this story: 'In January 1985, 52 peasants from Sesori, San Miguel, were arrested for investigation by the Arce Battalion, apparently on suspicion of supplying the guerrillas with food. They were interrogated in San Miguel on 16 January and subsequently an expert in "psychological warfare" gave them indoctrination talks ... They were shown films produced by the armed forces' psychological operations unit. After 72 hours they were ... returned by lorry to Sesori.'

43. Ibid.

44. *Inforpress*, 18 July 1985, p. 10.

45. *IHT*, 15 July 1985.

46. *IHT*, 8 July 1985.

47. See e.g. *Guardian*, 7 March 1985.

48. *Inforpress*, 18 July 1985.

Select Bibliography

Ageus, *Salud en El Salvador – Otra razón para el combate popular* (private publication, Costa Rica, 1981).

Alegría, Claribel and Flakoll, D.J., *Cenizas de Izalco* (Dirección de Publicaciones del Ministerio de Educación, El Salvador, 1976).

Alegría, Claribel and Flakoll, D.J., *No me agarran viva – La mujer salvadoreña en lucha* (Ediciones ERA, Mexico, D.F., 1983).

Armstrong, R. and Wheaton, P., *Reform and Repression – US Policy in El Salvador 1950–1981* (Solidarity Publications, San Francisco, California, USA, February 1982).

Bronstein, Audrey, *The Triple Struggle – Latin American Peasant Women* (War on Want Publications, London, England, 1982).

Camino, *El Salvador – Background to the Crisis* (Central American Information Office, Cambridge, Mass., USA, 1982).

Cayetano Carpio, Salvador, *Secuestro y Capucha* (Colección Debate, Editorial EDUCA, Costa Rica, 1979).

Cisneros, Rosa Judith, *La condición jurídica de la mujer salvadoreña* (Asociación Demográfica Salvadoreña, El Salvador, February 1976).

Committee of Professional Health Workers, *El Salvador – War and Health* (COMIN Publications, Nicaragua, April 1983).

Dalton, Roque, *(Las historias prohibidas del Pulgarcito* (Siglo XXI, Mexico, 1974).

Dalton, Roque, *Miguel Marmol* (Colección Seis, Editorial EDUCA, Costa Rica, 2nd edition, 1982).

Davies, Miranda, ed., *Third World – Second Sex* (Zed Press, London, England, 1983).

Dé Herrera, Norma, *El papel de la mujer en la revolución salvadoreña* (Editorial Claves Latinoamericanas, Mexico, D.F., September 1983).

Deighton, Jane, *et al.*, *Sweet Ramparts – Women in Revolutionary Nicaragua* (War on Want Publications, London, England, 1983).

Doljanin, Nicolas, *Chalatenango, La guerra descalza* (Editorial El Día, Mexico, D.F., 1982).

Dunkerley, James, *The Long War – Dictatorship and Revolution in El Salvador* (Junction Books, London, England, 1982; Verso Books, London, England, 1985).

Estudios Ecuménicos, *La mujer en el proceso ecuménico de liberación* (Estudios Ecuménicos No. 40, Centro de Estudios Ecuménicos A.C., Yosemite 45, México 18, D.F., 1980).

Federación de Trabajadores del Campo, *Los trabajadores del campo y la reforma agraria en El Salvador* (Universidad Autónoma de Guerrero, Mexico, 1982).

Gettleman, M., et al., *El Salvador – Central America in the New Cold War* (Grove Press, Inc., New York, USA, 1981).

Harris, Olivia, ed., *Latin American Women* (Minority Rights Group Report No. 57, London, England, 1983).

Keogh, Dermot, *Romero: El Salvador's Martyr* (Dominican Publications, Dublin, 1981).

Latin American and Caribbean Women's Collective, *Slaves of Slaves – The Challenge of Latin American Women* (Zed Press, London, England, 1980).

Lernoux, Penny, *Cry of the People* (Doubleday, New York, USA, 1980).

Martinez, Ana Guadalupe, *Las carceles clandestinas de El Salvador* (Colección Nuestro Continente, Universidad Autónomo de Sinaloa, Mexico, 1980).

Menjivar, Rafael, *Formación y lucha del proletariado industrial salvadoreño* (Colección Estructuras y Procesos, UCA, El Salvador, 1979).

Pearce, Jenny, *Under the Eagle – US Intervention in Central America and the Caribbean* (Latin American Bureau, London, England, 2nd edition, 1982).

Rogers, Barbara, *The Domestication of Women – Discrimination in Developing Societies* (Tavistock Publications, London, England, 1980).

Ventura, José, *El poder popular en El Salvador* (Editorial Mex-Sur, Mexico, D.F., 1983).

Wire, *Women and War – El Salvador* (Women's International Resource Exchange, 2700 Broadway, New York, 10025, USA, 1981).

The Commission for Human Rights of El Salvador (CDHES)

The CDHES was founded in 1978 in response to the increasing scale of human rights violations in El Salvador. It is a non-government organization and member of the International Federation of the Rights of Man (FIDH) and the Central American Commission for the Defence of Human Rights. It has consultative status in the United Nations. The CDHES is an humanitarian, non-denominational organization, which receives financial assistance from international human rights organizations and development agencies.

The work of the CDHES includes giving legal advice and assistance to political prisoners and families of the disappeared; recording and denouncing human rights violations at a national and international level and, as far as funds permit, helping victims of the repression in financial difficulties. The CDHES has offices in San Salvador, Mexico City and Managua and representatives in the United States and many European countries.